M000308162

COWS DON'T STAY MILKED

John Covington

"Cows Don't Stay Milked," by John Covington. ISBN 978-1-62137-951-5 (softcover); 978-1-62137-952-2 (hardcover); 978-1-62137-953-9 (eBook).

Published 2017 by Virtualbookworm.com Publishing Inc., P.O. Box 9949, College Station, TX , 77842, US.

TABLE OF CONTENTS

FOREWORD

JOHN COVINGTON'S LATEST BOOK, *Cows Don't Stay Milked*, is a must read for anyone who holds a leadership position or aspires to have one. He emphasizes that life is a journey. We must work at refining the characteristics that help us grow as better people and grow spiritually. By deliberately working hard to get better every single day, we will also grow as more effective leaders.

The qualities of a leader that Covington focuses on are the nine fruits of the Spirit identified in Galatians 5:22-23. Love, joy, peace, patience, kindness, goodness, faithfulness, gentleness, and self-control are the attributes that must be nourished on our journey to become better people and more effective leaders. To make his points, Covington devotes a chapter of the book for each of the spiritual fruits. He illustrates the importance of each in the life of a friend, a family member, or a colleague, followed by a similar example using a Biblical character whose story also adds clarity to the importance of the fruit.

John Covington is president of Chesapeake Consulting, Inc., a company he founded in 1988. Chesapeake Consulting works with companies around the globe to provide creative solutions customized to the unique business management problems the companies are facing.

I had the good fortune of being able to get to know John and his wife, Linda, when I served as provost and president of The

1

University of Alabama. John's undergraduate degree is in chemical engineering. In the years since he graduated, John has demonstrated time and time again that he is "faithful, loyal, firm, and true" to his alma mater. He is a Distinguished Fellow in both the Department of Chemical and Biological Engineering and the College of Engineering. He is Past National Chair of the Capstone Engineering Society. He has generously given of his time and talent to the students at the Capstone for decades.

The author of six books and renowned speaker on leadership development, Covington is recognized nationally as a mesmerizing storyteller. His down-to-earth and conversational writing style makes his books pleasurable reads. This book is very different from other books that focus on theoretical aspects of leadership. After reading *Cows Don't Stay Milked*, you will have insight into how to grow as a better person.

Judy Bonner

28th President

The University of Alabama

PREFACE

THIS IS A BOOK on improving your leadership. Many people who write about leadership, including me, are convinced we have a leadership crisis today. I am writing this book during the 2016 presidential campaign between Hillary Clinton and Donald Trump. This Sunday, our pastor said this election is like a divorce and a fight for the custody of the children—the American people being the children. The American people are saying, "We want to go live with grandma!"

I would not hire either of these two candidates to work at Chesapeake Consulting, and one of them is going to end up being president.

Donald Trump ended up winning this election, and I hope and pray he grows and evolves into the job so he can help bring us closer together as a nation.

When I was a young boy, the president of the United States was Dwight Eisenhower. President Eisenhower was a West Point graduate, a World War II hero, and was so well-liked and respected, his campaign buttons read "I Like Ike."

Following Eisenhower was John F. Kennedy, who was also a WW II hero, a Harvard graduate, young and full of charisma. Many of us remember his speech when he said, "Ask not what your country can do for you; ask what you can do for your country."

Yes, these men were flawed, just like all humans. However, it seems we, as a people, did not dwell on it as much as we do today. We spent more time focusing on the good traits.

These men, and many other men and women like them, were great role models.

In this book, I plan to lift up some behavior that we should try and emulate to enable us to focus on improving our leadership ability. If each of us makes an effort to improve what we do and not worry as much about the other person improving, then things will get better. It will be a better country and world in which to live.

One thing we will learn is that this improvement is an ongoing process. Several years ago, a young business owner asked me for some advice. "John, when does all of the chaos end in growing your business?" he asked.

My reply was, "When you die."

It is ongoing; it never ends.

I busted a gut laughing the first time I heard the term "Cows Don't Stay Milked." My good friend, Dr. Mike Umble, (of Baylor University) and I were in the process of trying to write a book, and Mike uttered that cow wisdom (my friend Keith Pugh said that I should say he "uddered" the wisdom). That wisdom applies to everything, from your workout regimen to your diet, spiritual life, and relationships. There are very few one-shot deals in life besides death.

Nothing stays the same; it either gets better or worse. If left to their own devices, things normally get worse. You cannot get in tip-top condition then sit on the couch and eat bonbons all month and think you will maintain your fitness. Cows do not stay milked.

The same principle applies to leadership with regard to making a difference in the world. That leadership word applies to all of us. Most everyone has some role of being a leader and doing something.

Even the best performers, who we admire with regard to making a difference, seem to slip into some sort of complacency at times. We need to continuously work on honing our skills.

Leaders who want to approach their potential must be spiritual folks who lead from a strong inner core. That core can be developed to the point of being good—but, as the title maintains, you have to keep the discipline of maintaining the core, as those ornery cows do not stay milked. You will never reach perfection, but you can maintain a positive trajectory.

Each of us can be better leaders by spending time and effort in becoming more spiritually mature or, as some might say, being on a path of spiritual formation. In fact, if you do not do that, I see no hope that you will ever evolve to the level of leadership that is possible for you. The sad thing is you will never know what you have missed.

We all need to become better leaders for the sake of those directly around us, the numerous others we touch, and for the future we will impact.

Let's see if together we can learn some stuff that will help us keep those cows milked.

John Covington

INTRODUCTION

BELOW IS A DIAGRAM of you as a leader that I first introduced in my book, <u>Enterprise Fitness</u>.

Chesapeake Leadership Model

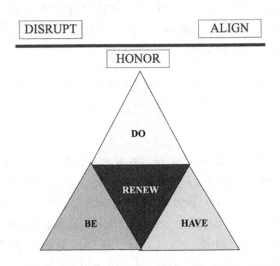

The parts of the triangle are Do, Have, Be and Renew. The "Do" is what is visible, and it is the action you should see a leader "Doing." Leaders should be "Disrupting" the system they are working in; while being "Disruptive," they should "Honor" those people involved. If you are going to "Disrupt" things, you also need to have both an overall plan and a method to your madness. There must be an "Alignment" element. You need a vision of what a new system will look like and how you will show people that vision.

The "Have" part of the triangle is your intuition and knowledge. It is what you have accumulated in the way of experience over the years. When we make judgments, we see something in reality; we compare it to our intuition and make a decision as to whether or not it is good or bad. When you put out effort to increase your knowledge and wisdom, your decision-making will improve.

The "Be" section has to do with your character. This "Be" section is the primary focus of this book.

The "Renew" section is the action plans one makes on an ongoing basis to achieve the improvement. Those are the procedures on how to milk the cows.

Here is an e-mail I received from my good friend, Mike Storms, when I sent several people the preface of the book and asked their opinion.

"John, I think it would be an awesome way to round out your pillars of leadership—align, disrupt, and honor. I have often thought that there should be a fourth pillar. I think it should be something that centers around the love for mankind, all people are equal, or just simply a love for life. We often have "leaders" who demonstrate the three basic pillars but push for a cause, world, and/or reality that divides, reinforces prejudice, hurts others, etc. The fact that you and I love dogs so much is because they have that basic instinct. They never feel sorry for themselves, and they forgive us and live each day with excitement and wonder. Imagine a well-trained dog with the ability to align, disrupt, and honor us humans around a cause or object. I suggest they have that fourth pillar that solidifies the perfect leadership style. If you can define, explain, and justify how love is a fourth pillar of leadership, I would buy the book. Good luck my friend, Mike."

I first met Mike when he was an engineer with Grove Manufacturing, a maker of cranes. Mike later went on to work with Manitowoc Crane, then Waukesha Engine, and finally, Elliott Turbine. I can recall one time I asked Mike what he wanted to do, and he told me he wanted to be head of operations. Well—he met his goal, as he is the head manufacturing person at Elliott and a darn good one. He is an excellent leader.

This was Mike's take on the book. It is not quite what I expected, but the more I pondered it, the more I realized that Mike had a better grasp of what I was trying to do than I did.

I do not think I have to add a "fourth pillar" as Mike calls it. Perhaps a deeper meaning for "Honor" will get the job done. We want to honor the person to the point of loving them. Isn't loving someone the ultimate way to honor them?

Other business leaders have the same thoughts as Mike. One of the better books I have read recently is *Everybody Matters* by Bob Chapman, who is the Chairman and CEO of Barry-Wehmiller. Chapman measures success by the impact that the organization has on people. He maintains that every business should be a "business family," with unconditional love, forgiveness, and nurturing.

This is a different mindset. This is not just idealism. Real companies and factories embrace this radical departure from traditional leadership and are having success both people-wise and profit-wise. I learned about Chapman's work from my friend,

Wayne Pitchford, who is the Vice President of Operations for Neptune in Tallassee, Alabama. Neptune has successfully embraced this different approach to leadership.

In this book, I am going to attempt to take us on a journey. Let me try and shed some insight on what I hope we experience.

I want to begin the journey with the understanding of how important humility is. I feel it is the core of leadership.

Next, I want us to ponder what we can control, and that is what we do with our time. We will see this near the beginning of the book when we talk about transitions, and at the end of the book when we discuss making the best of the moment. In transitions, we will reflect on the finite nature of our physical existence but how important that time can be in the future.

In the middle of the book, we will reflect and ponder on the behavior relating to the nine fruits.

Let us begin the trip!

CHAPTER ONE

Humility is the Key

JIM COLLINS, the famous author and management guru, made reference to a Level 5 Leader in his book, *Good to Great*. What Collins found in his research is that the most successful leaders are those who are humble. Humble does not mean weak—in fact, it means the opposite. In Richard E. Simmon's book, *The True Measure of a Man*, he says (on page 83), "Simply stated, life's greatest paradox can be summed up in the words, ***True strength is found in humility.***"

Throughout scripture, humility is lifted up: "For by the grace given me I say to every one of you: Do not think of yourself more highly than you ought, but rather think of yourself with sober judgement, in accordance with the measure of faith God has given you." Romans 12:3

Great figures of the Bible were known for their humility. *"Moses was more humble than anyone else."* Numbers 12:3 *" I, Paul, am God's slave."* Titus 1:1 And John the Baptist says, *"He must increase; I must decrease."* John 3:30.

In Luke, Jesus was telling a parable about how you should always select the seat reserved for people of a low position when going to a banquet. He ended the parable by saying: *"For everyone who exalts himself will be humbled, and he who humbles himself will be exalted."* Luke 14:11

A humble person is someone who does not think they are any better than anyone else. They are courteous, respectful, modest, and not proud.

Several years ago, Chesapeake Consulting did a lot of work for the Baltimore-Washington Conference of the United Methodist Church. The Bishop at the time was John Schol. At least once per quarter, Bishop Schol and I would have an hour-long chat. I loved my time with the Bishop, and we became great friends.

He once asked me, "What is the characteristic you think is the most valuable for a pastor?"

I did not hesitate; "Humility," I responded.

I based my answer solely on my experience of having observed five senior pastors at Severna Park United Methodist Church in Maryland. Of those five pastors, two of them were humble servants. The church prospered and grew under their leadership. The other three were all a legend in their own minds, bordering on arrogance. Membership declined on their watch. My guess is those three did not start off their ministry with a lack of humility. Obviously, their cows did not stay milked, and ego and self-centeredness took over their inner beings. The effects are predictable. Don't milk your cows, and you will pay the price— and so will those around you.

Humility will be found in those who have the Holy Spirit dwelling within them to the point where the Holy Spirit is in control most of the time.

If one obeys God's basic command, "love God, and love what God loves," the humility thing is an effect of that. That brings us back to what Mike was referring to in his e-mail—that love for humanity.

Loving your employees, or those in your sphere of influence, is the key to you growing as a more effective leader.

CHAPTER TWO

Our Transitions; the Cycle of Life and Death are Real

"'MEANINGLESS! MEANINGLESS!" Says the Teacher. 'Utterly meaningless! Everything is meaningless.' What does man gain from all his labor at which he toils under the sun? Generations come and generations go, but the earth remains forever. The sun rises and the sun sets, and hurries back to where it rises. The wind blows to the south and turns to the north; round and round it goes, ever returning on its course. All streams flow into the sea, yet the sea is never full. To the place the streams come from, there they return again. All things are wearisome, more than one can say. The eye never has enough of seeing, nor the ear its fill of hearing. What has been will be again, what has been done will be done again; there is nothing new under the sun. Is there anything of which one can say, 'Look! This is something new'? It was here already, long ago; it was here before our time. There is no remembrance of men of old, and even those who are yet to come will not be remembered by those who follow." Ecclesiastes 1: 2-11

Many of your loved ones have died. Many of your favorite pets have crossed over the rainbow bridge. The place where you worked for 25 years is abandoned, and weeds grow in the parking lot. Is the Teacher (Solomon) correct? Is it all meaningless?

Let us look at a few of these transitions, starting with one my dog had to endure. Then let's see if we can make some sense out of it.

Derrick the Duck

The nine-year-old German shepherd trotted towards the tee box on the 16th hole at Tall Pines golf course in Tuscaloosa, Alabama. She loved going on walks with her human, who she referred to as "Dad."

It was a brisk winter day, with frost on the ground. This weather reminded her of walks in Maryland, the state she had left just ten months ago. She loved the cold weather. She was especially fond of snow and "helping" Dad shovel the driveway and sidewalk in front of their suburban home. One of the many games she played was when he would throw a shovel full of snow, she would jump up to try and bite the snow. Her thick, black and tan coat was ideal for chilly weather. It seemed the colder it got, the younger she became and the more she frolicked like a puppy. The rare southern cold snap was a welcome relief to her.

She was a handsome animal and drew many compliments on how pretty and striking she was. She seemed to know it and carried herself with an air of confidence. Standing on the elevated tee box, she looked out over the pond, ears up and alert. She scanned from one end to the other, looking for her friend. He wasn't there today.

Derrick was a large duck, nearly as large as a swan. He was mostly black, with a few white feathers, and a white fluffy breast. Around both eyes, he had an unattractive red, bumpy patch of skin that looked almost like a rooster's beard. He was indeed an ugly duckling. What Derrick lacked in looks, he made up in personality. The houses that were close to the 15th fairway had adopted him as their neighborhood pet duck. Nearly five years

16

ago, he somehow got separated from the rest of his flock that spent their time on one of the holes on the front nine. Derrick may have been the smart one. He had all these people, and their attention, to himself.

They had met in April. Derrick was not afraid of people nor their dogs, most of which were lap dogs and much smaller than Derrick. When Maggie charged him that first time, he was in disbelief. An 85-pound German shepherd was different than a toy poodle. When only 20 yards separated the two animals, Derrick gave it all the energy he had, hoisted his overweight body about two inches off the ground, and flew the ten or so feet from the tee box to the pond. Splash!! In went Derrick. And splash—in went Maggie after him. That was the beginning of a friendship and an early morning ritual. Maggie was only allowed three swims until Dad figured out to hook up her leash when they were close to the 16th tee box. The two friends would have to communicate without a morning swim.

Three weeks earlier, Maggie was trotting down the 14th fairway towards the green. A creek separated the 14th and 15th fairway, and she was headed towards the wooden bridge to cross over. Dad, as usual, was lagging behind. She had caught a familiar scent in the air and was anxious to discover what it was. She had detected that scent only two times before, once searching for a dog that was found dead in the woods and the other on an assignment with the Maryland State Police looking for a lost woman. It was the smell of death.

She crossed the bridge and made a left towards the 15th green. There was a line of upper-middle-class houses along the right side of the fairway—the type of houses one would expect to be located on a golf course. She had seen Derrick near the houses on occasion, begging for bread. That was a long way from his safe haven on the pond. If something bad got between Derrick and that pond, he would be in danger. He was an excellent swimmer but a horrible aviator and slow afoot.

She made a beeline to where the smell was, about 15 yards past the ladies tee box. It was a critter she had never seen before. However, there was also the scent of another animal—one that was not dead but had been at the spot and had moved on. She needed Dad to come check this out and he had not yet crossed over the bridge.

Over years of search and rescue work (plus drug detection), communication between Maggie and her human was easy and natural. She stood over the critter and turned her head to give Dad a look as he crossed over to the 15th fairway. She would not move, sending a signal that he was to come investigate what she had found. It was not something mundane, such as another dog marking their territory. She would never bother him for that. It was something serious that he needed to see.

"You found a dead armadillo that has been partially eaten," he said.

Dead armadillos are normally found along Alabama roadsides, not in the middle of a golf course where no cars travel. This armadillo had met a violent death.

She renewed her trip to the pond, where she stopped within 50 yards, and her leash was snapped on. Derrick was there waiting, perched like some royalty between the two blue markers on the tee box. The animals did their normal silent communication, which appeared to be one out of mutual respect/affection.

Three days had passed since she discovered the armadillo. Dad took her leash off at the 13th par three that leads straight away into 14. That smell again… the one of death was fresh in the air. She went to the left of the fairway, close to the back of the pond. There was the sign of a struggle and the smell of that same animal she had detected at the site of the armadillo body. Again she stopped, turned towards Dad, and gazed. He would have to abandon his normal path to come investigate.

"Oh no, I think it is Derrick," he said. There were plenty of black feathers, a few white feathers, and plenty of white fuzz, the type that covered Derrick's breast. Dad walked up the embankment to the south bank of the pond, the one opposite from the 16th tee box. He came down from the embankment, shaking his head. Maggie had sensed a mood change in her handler, one of sadness.

"Come on, gal. Let's go." And he resumed his walk. She lagged behind. She recognized Derrick's scent. Maybe she could rescue him by tracking him down. But the scent remained only in the spot of violence. Some creature had carried the body away from that spot—there was no trail.

Dad got all the way to the crossover bridge, and she was still lagging back, sniffing Derrick's feathers. He was nearly 400 yards away. "Maggie come!" it was a sterner call this time.

Have to go, she thought.

She caught up to him on the 15th fairway. As she approached the tee box for number 16, she stopped and waited for him to attach her leash as always. He didn't.

She climbed atop the tee box, looking for her friend.

He was not there. He was gone and will never be back again.

For several days, she continued looking. No longer—she now walks on by, looking for something else to amuse her.

Steve McCloskey

Victor McCloskey was the dad of my best friend, Steve. He was a tall man, balding and always with a smile on his face. Steve referred to his parents as George Burns and Gracie Allen, after the famous comedy couple. It was around 1965 in Springfield, Virginia. I was a teenager—out driving around. Why not swing by Stephen's house? I asked myself.

He hated for me to call him Stephen—more the reason to do it.

"Good evening, Mr. McCloskey. May I speak with Steve?" I asked.

A smile, or perhaps a grin, surfaced on Victor's face. "Well, John, that would be hard. You see, Steve is at a pizza party—with you." Mr. McCloskey replied.

There was a hint of a chuckle in his voice. Mr. McCloskey found humor in everything, and I had just given him a gift.

Steve was busted. This was before the days of cell phones, and teenagers used smoke signals to communicate. There was no way I could give Steve a heads up. Stephen was grounded—again. One of the clauses in Mr. McCloskey's last will and testimony was that Stephen's grounding sentences were terminated, and he was a free man at age 47 or so.

After high school, we stayed in touch, although always separated by great distance. Steve and his wonderful wife, Ann, visited Linda and me when we lived in North Carolina. Our North Carolina neighbors later told us they had never heard so much laughter coming from a house before.

When I was on business in Chicago, I was able to visit them, and I remember going to a track meet to watch their oldest daughter,

Jennifer. It was cold and rainy, and somehow, Stephen managed to stay in a warm, comfortable office while Ann and I weathered the elements and watched Jen zoom to victory. Each time I saw him, it was like we had never been separated.

Steve flew into Chattanooga, Tennessee when we lived there. At the time, he worked for an ad agency that was involved with Ronald McDonald. Steve had some hilarious Ronald McDonald stories. When I was trying to explain all of this to my young daughter, Leigh, she was convinced that Ronald McDonald was coming to visit us. She never got over the fact that Steve looked like Steve, rather than dressed up in a yellow costume with a red nose and big shoes.

On April 22nd of 2016, my cell phone rang. It was some oddball number I had never seen before, but I already knew who it had to be. "Hey John, it's Steve McCloskey—happy birthday!"

How did he always remember? He always called me on my birthday. It was a special thing he did. It would not take long to start reminiscing about old times, and we would both be in uncontrollable laughter. That moment was so special because he took the time to make it so.

In June of that same year, I was checking Facebook on my iPhone—something that my wife, Linda, despises. I guess it was the shock on my face that caused her to pause before she chided me for the infraction.

"Steve McCloskey died." As I read the post from his daughter, I was in disbelief.

As the Facebook posts continued for several days, I learned that calling people on their birthday was one of the things he did and enjoyed. Everyone commented on how special those birthday calls from Steve were.

On April 22nd 2017, there will be one less phone call. Stephen will not call. He's not there. He will never call again.

DuPont and Sherwin-Williams

"Where are all the fork truck drivers?" I asked. It was in June of 1985, and I had just taken over as plant manager of the Sherwin-Williams Baltimore site.

"They have to go back to jail on the weekends," one of the shift foremen replied.

As I toured through the packaging area, I noticed several of the machines were not running. I headed towards the maintenance shop to check on their status. The bad news was the mechanics were drinking beer on the job. The good news was at least they were supervised, as their boss was drinking with them.

We had 66 underground storage tanks that were leaking and had to be removed. This was an environmental nightmare and had to be corrected.

I quickly learned the guys dressed in the red sweatsuits were the plant drug dealers. The place was an absolute mess. If I wanted to mow tall grass, this was the place to be.

Sherwin-Williams had purchased the facility from Baltimore Paint and Chemicals, essentially to gain access to the Dutch Boy brand. At one time, Baltimore Paint and Chemicals had four plants: Los Angeles, Chicago, Philadelphia, and Baltimore. Los Angeles, Chicago, and Philadelphia had already been closed, and Baltimore was on thin ice. They had gone through several plant managers in Baltimore, and the facility was still not performing to bare minimum standards. I was probably the last shot.

The facility was old, poorly lit, and dingy. Located near the inner harbor of Baltimore, it butted up against a housing project. During the 1968 Civil Rights riots, the area was mostly in flames. It was a rough neighborhood. For the most part, the employees reflected the location.

The vast majority of the employees wanted the site to do well. They were good, hardworking folks. The place just lacked leadership and a direction. I wanted them to be successful. I sensed they knew that and were willing to get on board with new ideas.

One of the first things I did as plant manager was to implement the DuPont STOP program, which was a safety program based on attitude change. For years, DuPont was the recognized leader in industrial safety. Not only did the safety record at our Baltimore plant improve, that attitude carried over to other areas, such as quality, on-time performance, and cost controls. The facility ended up excelling in many areas and is still operating 30 years later.

Let me flash back to January of 1973—twelve years earlier. I was a young process engineer at DuPont's Photo Products plant in Brevard, North Carolina. The plant was nestled in the midst of 12,000 acres of mountain forest. At the time, we were the only DuPont plant with our own forest ranger. I can recall one safety meeting where the forest ranger came into the room and tossed a couple of rattlesnakes on the floor. The meeting topic was how not to get bit by a snake. That made a lasting impression—and no one got bit by a snake.

On one of my first days on the job, I got called to task by one of the chemical operators for putting my foot up on a board to tie my shoe. I had violated a safety rule. It seemed trivial and petty. Later, I learned that it was not—it was part of the DuPont approach to safety. Learning the ins and outs of a very successful industrial safety program was a big deal for me and served me well in my career. It certainly served all of those folks well, who otherwise may have been injured on the job.

I left DuPont in June of 1974 to go to work for Stauffer Chemicals.

Later, that DuPont plant was sold to a private investor. Today in 2016, that plant no longer exists, and the entire area has gone back to forest. The DuPont plant in Brevard is no longer there.

Transitions—one day you are here, the next day you are not. One day the plant is here, the next day it is not. What legacy do we leave?

Was it the overall plan of God for the Sherwin-Williams facility to survive? I don't know. I can only assume so. The plant was a gnat's rear end away from being shut down. When I took over the facility, there was already a team from our corporate office in Cleveland making plans to eliminate the site. The knowledge I gained from the DuPont experience was paramount in saving the Baltimore site. So although the DuPont site no longer exists, its legacy lived on in the form of helping to save the Sherwin-Williams facility. And I was just one person. How many others from that facility went on to other jobs and used their knowledge gained at Brevard to make a difference elsewhere?

So maybe it's not all meaningless. Will specific individuals be remembered? Probably not, so Solomon nailed that one when he said, "There is no remembrance of men of old, and even those who are yet to come will not be remembered by those who follow."

Not many of us are going to have a monument or statue to record our memory.

However, our individual lives in the present are affected and, in turn, will affect others. So in God's overall scheme of things, our individual actions are important and so live on. Neither our possessions nor anything we own lives on, only how we impact other people. Everything else is meaningless, and that is what the teacher was talking about.

Discussion Questions:

1. Write down three people who you knew that have died. What did they do that still impacts you today?
2. What else did they teach you?
3. Name and discuss a school, institution, company, or organization that no longer exists that still has an impact today.

CHAPTER THREE

The Holy Spirit and the Fruits of that Spirit

WHO IS THE HOLY SPIRIT?

If I claim that your potential is limited by whether or not you have the Holy Spirit dwelling within you, then perhaps we need to identify this person.

I am lucky and very fortunate. It seems that whenever I am working on some sort of a project, this Holy Spirit fellow pops in and helps me. That is what happened in the writing of this book. Our pastor, Chris Hodges, recently preached on the Holy Spirit, so I am going to tap into the knowledge he gave us.

First of all, the Holy Spirit is not an "it," it is a "He," and He is also on earth, whereas God and Jesus are in heaven. The Holy Spirit puts the wind in your sails and is your comforter. He is that inner voice that speaks up when you come home from work in a bad mood, and when you are starting to say something nasty, the ole Holy Spirit taps you on the shoulder and says something to the effect, "I don't think I would do that if I were you."

The Holy Spirit is also your teacher, guide, and friend. Have you ever gotten that nudge to step outside your comfort zone and to do something really cool for others or to expand your own horizon? Yep, that was Him.

The Old Testament refers to the Spirit in Isaiah 30:21 "Whether you turn to the right or to the left, your ears will hear a voice behind you saying, 'This is the way; walk in it.'"

In John 14:16-17, Jesus describes the Holy Spirit: "I will ask the Father, and he will give you another advocate to help you and be with you forever—the Spirit of truth. The world cannot accept him, because it neither sees him nor knows him. But you know him, for he lives with you and will be in you."

I am an early riser, and as part of my morning routine, I get outside and do some sort of exercise. Eons ago, I used to jog. I believe those days are over; now I go for long walks, and I normally have a dog with me. Occasionally while walking, I would come upon trash that someone has dropped, and I would get a nudge to pick it up. At times, I ignored the urge and walked on, but the urge was so great that I would turn around, go back, and get the garbage. Even Maggie, the dog, got into the act, as she would pick up discarded, plastic drink bottles and then drop them in front of our recycle bin at home.

Many times I would say (guessing I was talking to the Holy Spirit), "What difference does it make? Tomorrow, some teenager standing at this bus stop is going to throw another candy wrapper down, so what is accomplished by picking this up this morning?" I guess I was being somewhat of a stubborn and bratty child in the Father's eyes.

As I was walking back home on Rustling Oaks in Shipley's Choice subdivision in Millersville, Maryland, there was a smashed pumpkin in the middle of the road. It was a day or so after Halloween. The old nudge came to urge me to clean up that mess, as it was going to get worse as soon as cars started coming by. I picked up the pieces and placed them alongside the road. Several weeks later, a lady stopped me on my walk. I had never met this woman. She wanted to tell me what a great example I was for her children by picking up trash and specifically, that pumpkin. I would never have known that unless that woman had stopped and taken the time to tell me. The Spirit works in strange ways.

As with any other friend, teacher, or guide, you need to be in a relationship with the Spirit. Ask the Spirit to show you stuff and new things. Ask Him to help you to understand better. Ask Him to fill in the blank when you are stumped on something.

Ask the Spirit to change you for the better and to fill you. God has more for you to do. Be bold like Jabez, who (in 1 Chronicles 4:9-10) prayed these words: *"Oh, that You would bless me indeed, and enlarge my territory, and that Your hand would be with me, and that You would keep me from evil, that I may not cause pain."* Ask a blessing for yourself and ask for more responsibility to make a difference for others.

You cannot rest on your laurels. Remember, those cows do not stay milked.

To end our discussion on the Holy Spirit, I thought our pastor ended on a good note. Pastor Chris gave us the following quote: "Being filled with the Holy Spirit doesn't make me better than you; it makes me better than me."

And that is what this book is all about. It is to help you become a better you. That is important so you can continue to make a positive impact in your space during the time you have available.

Let us now begin to ease on over to look at the fruits of the Spirit as outlined in Galatians. In the following chapters, I will begin with a quote from the gifted author, Max Lucado, and his description of the fruits in his book, <u>Grace for the Moment</u>. The purpose of this exercise is to give the reader an idea of what this behavior looks like with real, everyday people like you and me.

If we embrace this charge, then the Holy Spirit will dwell within us, and we will be a new or (at least) an improving creation.

The visible proof of this improvement will be in showing the fruits of the Spirit, as outlined in Galatians 5:22-23, which are *love, joy, peace, patience, kindness, goodness, faithfulness, gentleness and self-control.* We can judge a tree by the fruit that it bears.

So, if you would, please go stand in front of your mirror and judge for yourself how you are doing. I am going to attempt to give you some comparison reflections to help you.

For each of the fruits, I am going to choose some friends and some Biblical characters for you to use, as a comparison, to help you in your tasks of comparing your behavior to these spiritual fruits. The friends I choose are all people who are serious about their relationship with God. They are not saints by any stretch of the imagination. However, all such people (people who take their faith seriously) are going to reflect these fruits at some level.

The fruits are not like spiritual gifts, where everyone has different gifts. All serious believers should exhibit all of the nine fruits—at least some of the time. This is a high standard that we will never really meet perfectly. We do want to make progress, though.

I experienced some resistance with some of those I wanted to use as examples. Many times, humility can lead to not wanting a light shined on what you have done. One of the arguments I have used with some of my friends is that it is not about them. It is about what the Holy Spirit has done, and they were merely vehicles. That might take humility to a deeper level, as it should.

Try not to be too hard on yourself. Other than Christ, all of the other folks who assume roles in the Bible are just like us—good old folks that mess up a bunch but might occasionally get it right. If you find someone who has perfectly aced all of these fruits, then one of two things has happened; either you are dead and have met your maker, or you are experiencing the second coming of Christ. No one is going to display these fruits entirely.

I think a water and oil analogy is appropriate. Let's say that water is God-centered, and oil is self-centered. We all have a certain level of water and oil. Our goal is to increase the water level, and by doing, so we push out some oil.

Note that Max Lucado uses the term "I choose" at the beginning of each one of the fruits. I think that is critically important to absorb. The reflection of a fruit starts off by being a choice. A choice is something we all can control.

Discussion Questions:

1. Explain why relying on the Holy Spirit for decision making is better than going on our own judgement?
2. How do you know when your judgement is in alignment with what the Holy Spirit would want?
3. What level of discomfort is involved in yielding to the Spirit when your intuition tells you otherwise?

CHAPTER FOUR

Love

"I CHOOSE LOVE. No occasion justifies hatred; no injustice warrants bitterness. I choose love. Today I will love God and what God loves." Max Lucado, *Grace for the Moment.*

Ralph Stokes

"Hey, Linda. Wake up; it's Ralph." This conversation was routine in the late 1970s early 1980s, when Linda and I lived in Chattanooga, Tennessee. Ralph was our good friend and former University of Alabama football player. My wife, Linda, was founder of the Chattanooga chapter of the University of Alabama alumni club and had "bugged" Ralph Stokes to be involved. As Linda normally gets up at the crack of noon, Ralph took great pleasure in calling her before that time to talk club business. It seemed to help make his day.

We do not accumulate too many really great friends in life. Ralph and his lovely wife, Debra, are such friends for Linda and me. Sometimes we take our friends for granted. Their role of "friend" supersedes anything else they may be. That can be a mistake. We might miss a learning opportunity.

On one of my business trips to Atlanta, I spent the night with Ralph and Debra. Ralph likes to talk and play golf. Since I am an awful golfer, and it was too late to play, Ralph talked and I listened. I enjoy that. Ralph is interesting, and he has great stories—especially some involving an earlier time, when he was one of the first African-Americans to play football at the University of Alabama. Ralph was preparing a speech he was to give for Kennesaw University School of Business, and he was bouncing some of his ideas/stories off of me. I am going to share some of these stories with you, as I feel there is some valuable learning for us in them.

It was the early 1970s, and Ralph was the most highly sought after running back in the nation. He was "Mr. Football" in the state of Alabama and was fresh from scoring the winning touchdown in the state championship game for Robert E. Lee High School in Montgomery. For those of you who remember the movie, "Remember the Titans," a story about an all-black high school merging with an all-white one, Ralph said he lived that experience. The University of Alabama had already broken the color barrier a year earlier with defensive end, John Mitchell. The legendary coach, Paul "Bear" Bryant, had his eye on Ralph and wanted him to play for the Crimson Tide.

Ralph told Coach Bryant that he probably would not go to Alabama because his mother heard Bear say he would not recruit black players. Coach Bryant was not used to taking no for an answer, so off he went to Montgomery to meet Mrs. Stokes. The meeting did not start off well for the coach.

Mom: "Coach, didn't you say you would never recruit a black player?"

Coach: "Yes, and I meant it. And I was wrong."

Ralph said this is a great teaching point to the kids at Kennesaw—own it!! If you did it or said it, own it. Coach Bryant owned it.

Mom: "Who is going to take care of Ralph when he is at school?"

Coach: "I will. I will be his father away from home."

Mom: "Who is going to be with him when he walks across campus and people say mean things to him?"

Coach: "No one. If I did not think he could handle it, I would not be here."

Mom: "Will you treat my son the same as others?"

Coach: "No. I will treat your son fair."

Later, Ralph's Mom came into the living room and said, "Ralph, it's your decision, but if I were you, I would go to Alabama and play football for that man!"

Two other great African-American players were in that same recruiting class, Sylvester Croom and Mike Washington. Both Sylvester and Mike went on to play in the National Football League, and (when he was hired at Mississippi State) Sylvester was the first African-American head coach in the Southeastern Conference.

Football players got to register early. It was Ralph's first semester, and he had to pick a major. Many of his white friends were picking business, and that also appealed to Ralph, so business it was.

However, one of the assistant coaches stepped in and said, "Ralph, you cannot major in business. How about social science or P.E.?"

Ralph replied, "But, Coach, I want to major in business."

The assistant prevailed and said, "If you want to change this, you are going to have to get it approved through Coach Bryant."

Ralph entered Bryant's office. "Ralph, I understand you want to major in business. Why?"

Ralph replied, "My Daddy goes to work with his name on his shirt. I want to wear a suit and tie to work."

Bryant replied, "Good enough for me."

Later, Ralph was told that he was such a high-profile recruit, they did not want to run the risk of him flunking out. They did not know my friend and his work ethic very well.

In the first semester of Ralph's sophomore year, he was walking out of the cafeteria with his head down and ran slap into Coach Bryant, who quickly had his forefinger in Ralph's chest, poking him and raising Cain.

"I just got off the phone with your mother. I assured her this was unacceptable and it would NOT happen again." Coach said.

Ralph was clueless as to what had happened.

Coach continued, "You got a C in marketing! That is your major. There is no excuse for this. It will not happen again. Do you understand?"

Coach Bryant had gotten the report card before Ralph and had already called Mom. Ralph's message to the student's: "He said he would be my dad away from home, and he was."

Later that year, Mike Washington, Sylvester Croom, and Ralph went together to meet with coach for a special request. The team had a rule of no facial hair. These three black players wanted a waiver on that.

"Coach, in the African-American community, it is important for a young man to have a mustache as a sign of manhood. Can we grow a mustache?"

Coach Bryant replied, "Is that why you are in my office? Get out of here—the answer is no!"

The next year, Bryant summoned the three players to his office for no particular reason. Washington and Croom were pretty well-behaved, so (of course) they blamed Ralph.

"What have you done? How come we are in trouble with coach?" Sylvester and Mike asked.

Ralph pled ignorance.

When they entered, Bryant said, "Last year, you guys came in here and wanted mustaches. I have since done some checking around. I have talked with John McKay at Southern Cal, Ara Parseghian at Notre Dame, and others. You can grow your mustaches. And also, none of the white players can grow one."

Ralph's lesson to the students: "He treated people fair but not the same." Coach fulfilled all of the promises made to his mother.

Although Ralph was the crown jewel of his recruiting class, he did not go on to the NFL. A series of injuries put a halt to his career as a football pro. Thank heavens he had that business degree.

Ralph went to work for a large insurance company located in Chattanooga. After his training, he was to be assigned to the field. However, no regional manager would take him because he was black. Finally, a fellow in South Carolina said, "Send him to me." He was a former Ku-Klux-Klan member.

I have heard Ralph say many times, "I am not going to allow you to hate me."

Today, he and the former Klan leader are best of friends. A heart changed. How can that happen?

Ralph moved up the ladder to a regional manager. He had a sales call in Georgia, and his boss said, "Ralph, you don't need to go on this call as the guy is a racist, and he will not buy from you."

Ralph insisted anyway and took one of his new white employees. At the meeting, the prospect would not shake hands with Ralph and directed all of his questions to Ralph's white subordinate. Of course, since the subordinate did not know anything, Ralph answered the questions. Ralph was not well-prepared for the meeting, and they did not get the sale—just as Ralph's boss had predicted.

"See, I told you he was a racist, and that is why he did not buy from you," the boss said.

"He might be a racist. I don't know. But that is not the reason he did not buy from us. The reason he did not buy from us is I was unprepared and did not answer the questions properly," Ralph replied.

Ralph's message to the students: "Own it" (verse #2).

Another situation developed in Tennessee with the same scenario—a racist prospect. Ralph's boss tried to keep him from going, but (again) he was adamant and took his token white subordinate. Same exact beginning—no handshake for Ralph, direct questions to the white guy, and Ralph answering them. But this time, he answered them well. Meeting was over.

Client got up, looked Ralph square in the eye, put out his hand, and said, "I am buying insurance from you!"

I liked Ralph the minute I met him, and we have been close friends since the early 1980s. At one time, Ralph worked for Chesapeake as our sales and marketing director. We have had many conversations—mostly Ralph telling cool stories and me listening. I never overtly bring up the issue of race. I don't love Ralph because of his color; I love Ralph for who he is. However, sometimes the topic of race comes up, and he has lived experiences I will never understand. I most recall him saying the phrase "I am not going to allow you to hate me" in regard to his own issues with race.

In preparing to write this book, I popped Ralph a note. I reminded him of his comment. Since he said he was not going to allow the person to hate him, I asked if that meant he chose to love the person.

He replied, "I choose to love."

As an African-American, he chose to love this former KKK leader before he had ever met him. That is putting aside assumptions and looking at this person as a child of God, who is loved by God.

Ralph chose to love what God loves. We all get it right sometimes. Ralph got this one right.

Jonah

My name is Jonah. After you get done hearing my story, you will probably think I am the exact opposite of Ralph Stokes, who chose to love a former Ku-Klux-Klan member and ended up changing a heart. Unfortunately, I did the opposite. However, there is a huge learning opportunity sometimes in watching the way not to do things.

I came from a humble background—the son of a tent maker. I was an apprentice prophet under Amos and ended up with a really neat job as prophet during the realm of Jeroboam.

Jeroboam and I focused on purging out false gods and getting Samaria, which is in Israel, back on track with their relationship with the real God—the one of Abraham, Isaac, and Jacob.

God was pleased with us, and Israel began to experience some military victories over our enemies again. Even the much hated and despised region of Nineveh was beginning to look like a potential target for us. Oh how much satisfaction we would have gotten by destroying those bloodthirsty heathens. Every Hebrew hated them.

I don't know about you, but when things are going too well, I always cringe a bit, waiting for something bad to happen. Life was good. I had a high status with the king and all of the luxurious living that comes along with that role—the finest housing and food, plus I was hanging out with the in-crowd. What could go wrong?

"Go to the great city of Nineveh and preach against it because its wickedness has come up before me," I heard a voice say.

I was certainly hoping it was just a bad case of indigestion—perhaps too much Italian food. But it was God.

"Are you kidding me?" I thought. I could not believe my ears.

No one hated Nineveh as much as I did. I was so looking forward to slaughtering them and getting revenge for all of the woes they have caused others. It is only right that they should pay and pay dearly.

With my luck, they are going to listen to my preaching and then repent, and God will spare them. That is not what I wanted.

I decided to disobey God, which (by the way) is never a good course of action. Instead of going to Nineveh, I decided to head to Tarshish, which is the exact opposite direction. I boarded a ship in Joppa, and off I went.

I was pretty happy with myself that I was not going to come to the aid of those savages. However, remember my advice in the previous statement on not disobeying God? Well, here is what happened.

Not long after we set sail—more than a long swim away from shore—a horrible storm came up. It was so severe that even the experienced sailors were crying out of fear. I was exhausted, probably a lot from anxiety, and I was somehow able to fall asleep down below decks. The ship was tossed about like a match box. Soon, the captain of the ship came to my bed and awoke me. He demanded that I go topside with everyone else who was braving the storm.

When I arrived on deck, what I saw was pure panic. They were throwing cargo off the ship and crying out to their own gods. Nothing was working. They drew lots to see who was the one causing this trouble, and I drew the shortest straw. I had to come clean. I admitted that I had disobeyed my God. As much as I hated to admit it, the only way to save the ship was for them to sacrifice me and throw me overboard. I figured that I was going to die anyway, so I begged them to throw me over the side.

Reluctantly, they tossed me overboard. Almost instantly, the sea calmed; the ship righted itself and sailed away—leaving me to tread water.

I watched the ship until it eventually disappeared over the horizon. What had I done? Why had I disobeyed? I pondered how long I could tread water before I succumbed to the sea and drowned.

I was losing strength. Then something bumped me hard from under the water. A new fear struck. Drowning was one thing, but being eaten alive by some sea creature was horrifying. The monster made another pass at me as if it were testing me for a menu item. When it passed by, I saw that it was over 70 feet long. This time it hit me harder.

A minute or so went by, and then I saw it coming back for what looked to be the kill. The monster was black on top and was 6-8 feet across. The bottom of its sizable mouth was white. As it neared, its head came out of the water, and before I knew it, I was heading headfirst into its stomach. The fish swallowed a large gulp of water, which washed me the rest of the way down into its belly.

I was hot, there was total darkness, and I was slimy. I knew that being swallowed by this monster was God's will. He delivered me from drowning. I pondered what was in store for me. Many thoughts were racing through my head.

I was in that fish monster for three days. Jesus actually referred to my three days in the fish in one of his teaching sessions. As much as I had preached for others to repent, now I was the one who needed to repent and ask forgiveness. My relationship with God deepened over the three days, and I was committed to doing what

God had asked me to do in the first place—go to Nineveh and preach.

God had the fish vomit me, his rebellious prophet, onto the shore. My friends, this was not a pretty sight. I was covered in fish yak, and I smelled worse than awful. I spent some time getting cleaned up, and off to Nineveh I went, which was still a good three days off.

My hatred for the Ninevites was rekindled when I met their king. However, I delivered the message, as my God had instructed. The message was that unless they repented, they would be destroyed in 40 days.

Much to my chagrin and displeasure, the people of Nineveh repented, and (of course) God spared them.

I am embarrassed about my earthly behavior. After God spared these poor people, not only did I not rejoice and join in praise and celebration, I actually pouted. Here is a direct quote that I spoke to God (I am so ashamed):

"I knew that you are a gracious and compassionate God, slow to anger and abounding in love, a God who relents from sending calamity. Now, O Lord, take away my life, for it is better for me to die than to live." Jonah 4:2b-3

Are you kidding me? What a jerk I was. I did not have the loving spirit of Ralph Stokes, who chose to love. I, in my weakness, chose to be self-centered.

Please choose to be like Ralph.

Comments:

In many books, you have to wait to the end to get the punch line. Here, we are at the motherlode. Love—right here at the get-go.

You know something—it is hard. It is easy to love those people who love us or to love someone who you just like. But here, we are asking Ralph Stokes to love a former Ku-Klux-Klan member, or a racist. We are asking Jonah to love the people from Nineveh, who are his enemies. We are asking you to love that employee that you can't stand or that boss who treats you like crap. We are asking you to love the vendor that has cheated you or the person who makes snide comments about your weight.

This is a big task, and it is not easy. I have found it to be one of the more difficult things in my career to do. But intellectually, I know that it must be done, and I also know that it is a proactive and deliberate action. It is a choice.

I have learned that you must test and challenge assumptions to be able to love. Let me explain.

Over nearly three decades of running a business, I have had a lot of employees travel through here. Most have left because that is sort of the nature of the business and what I have set up. Most have moved on to better things after having spent time at Chesapeake, learning new things, making contacts, and perhaps regaining some confidence. Thank heavens several key people have been here for a long time, giving us some stability and some old farts for me to hang around with.

Some people have left on good terms, and some have not. I have had people leave, go into competition with us, and use our materials (of course, they took our name off of the materials). And some continued client relationships they had when they were on our payroll. They didn't see anything wrong with that. If you have that happen to you a few times, you can develop a case of paranoia.

Do you not trust people and try to micro-manage every client relationship, or do you let the consultant try and reach their potential by not micro-managing them? That case of paranoia can adversely affect your relationships with other employees. I have always attempted to err on the trust side. Many times, that takes additional effort and thought on my part.

A case in point—I had received some information about an employee that did not look good on the surface. However, I had never had any reason before to doubt that employee; I trusted him. Nevertheless, I was feeling uneasy. I was uneasy to the point that I needed to sit down with my little self and say, "Hey, this person has always been loyal, and I choose to continue to love this person. I must be missing something." I had to make the assumption that what I "saw" was wrong. And that was my mindset.

I never said anything to the employee—thank heavens. That would have been awful, to have even approached the topic. It certainly would have sent a signal back to this employee that there was a lack of trust. Later, I learned through conversations that it was perfectly innocent, what I had seen. I gave myself a mental high-five. If I had made a big deal out of it, I would have caused a problem where one did not exist. The point is, I had to do a mental exercise of love and ignore my assumptions. It was like psyching myself out. It was a proactive and deliberate exercise, one that Jonah should have gone through.

Loving someone does not mean you need to accept poor workmanship or performance. In fact, if you love someone, you want that person to be successful. Are they in the right job? Do they need a change? Sometimes loving someone (and all the others in your organization) may mean you need to terminate their employment. However, here is a head's up. If you terminate someone's employment, you may love him, but do not get upset if that love is not returned.

Discussion Questions:

1. List three people in your current sphere of influence who you do not like or you have trouble trusting.
2. List the things about them that you like and admire. What does God see in those people?
3. What assumptions did you make about those people that caused you to dislike them? Are those assumptions valid?
4. How would your culture change if you treated everyone as if they were related to you?
5. Make a list of those people in your immediate sphere of influence. They may be family members, employees, peers, etc. What would it be like if you prayed for them at least once per week?

CHAPTER FIVE

Joy

"I CHOOSE JOY. I will invite my God to be the God of circumstance. I will refuse the temptation to be cynical…the tool of the lazy thinker. I refuse to see people as anything less than human beings, created by God. I will refuse to see any problem as anything less than an opportunity to see God." Max Lucado, *Grace for the Moment.*

The Guys at Bibb County Correctional Facility

Jimbo, Worth, Robert, and I had just arrived. The meeting was 30 minutes late in starting, as the facility had a lockdown because the head count did not add up. That is a bad thing in a prison.

For the second week in a row, the air-conditioner was not working, and it was July in central Alabama. The sleeping quarters were not even air-conditioned, and the facility was overcrowded. It's a prison—it was supposed to be miserable, right? There is a GED program but no vocational education. No one wants to be in prison.

Lockdown and dinner were complete, and the inmates began to file in. We have had a high of over 150 attend the small group sessions when the air-conditioning was working. Attendance was now probably down to 120.

As the men were filing in, they would beam smiles at our presence. Almost everyone made eye contact, acknowledging us with a smile and a point of a finger. Many came over for handshakes, a fist bump, or a hug. It was genuine. They were happy to be involved in this study and happy to see us. It was a warm environment. It is one of the highlights of my week. I love those guys.

There was about a ten to fifteen-minute time frame where the groups were getting set up, chairs were getting moved around, and there was some general chaos of getting organized. The inmates ran almost the entire program. All of the small group facilitators were inmates. We were there to mentor, to add some thoughts. However, I think being there was the big thing.

Our leader, Jimbo, always said, "You can't fake showing up." It meant something.

During the chaos time, Joe, who looked to be in his early 40's, was talking about his week, and the conversation was laced with scripture verses. Worth and I were listening to him. What got me was the joy that was evident in Joe. It was to the point I felt a tad blown away. I wanted to say something to Worth about it, but we had to get the program going. It was Worth's week to begin with an opening statement. Then we broke off into our groups.

I went and joined Kenny's group. I was with them last week and started them on doing a prayer list for one another, so I wanted to follow-up on how that was going. As we reviewed the lesson, I was struck again by the joy we felt in the room.

Kenny proudly said, "When I get out of here, I am going to run a small group at the Church of the Highlands."

He said this in a manner that made me think he was going to get out very soon.

"So when do you get out?" I asked.

With a proud smile on his face, he said, "Only eight years."

Joy—"I will invite my God to be the God of circumstance." I am humbled to the core by the attitude I witnessed. I wasn't the only one.

It was getting close to our time to leave, and Worth was giving his wrap-up after each small group had orally reported to the larger group on how they were doing.

"I continue to be amazed at the joy I feel in here, given these circumstances. I don't think I could do what you guys do," Worth said.

Worth verbalized what I was thinking but did a much better job.

These men had made bad choices in their lives. That is why they are in prison.

This particular group of men was not like the general prison population. Everyone in the prison population had one thing in common—they had made bad choices, which (more than likely) harmed others. The difference with many of these men is they had asked the Lord Jesus to dwell within them, to be part of their lives, and to guide them. Although they were in the same exact environment as the other inmates, they chose to find joy in their circumstances.

In October of the same year, I was facilitating a small group of five inmates in a study. I asked each to tell the story of their individual spiritual journey. Some of the men told what they did to be in prison; about the same number chose not to tell. It seemed drugs were at the root of a lot of the issues—either being hooked on drugs and needing to steal to support their habit, or dealing drugs, as doing such provided what appeared to be a good income. One of my five had been convicted of murder, as someone died during the drug issues and he got the blame for it. Another was a medical doctor who chose not to disclose his crime, another a former high school football star who had a scholarship offer to play quarterback for Florida State, and another a notorious burglar who made statewide news when his case was solved.

The personal testimonies were heart-wrenching, and there was dead silence after each one. After the last man had finished, the man convicted of murder spoke out. "Is it just me or does anyone else feel grateful to be in this prison?"

I could not believe what I was hearing.

The rest of the men were agreeing and saying they would probably be dead if it were not for prison.

They had found peace and freedom in a place that is supposed to take away your freedom.

These particular inmates at Bibb County Correctional facility chose to be joyful, and they were joyful.

Paul

My name is Paul. You may know me as the Apostle Paul. I wasn't always so "apostle"-acting, though. Let me explain.

I was born a good Jewish boy in Rome during the time of the Roman Empire. My parents named me Saul, so Paul was a name change for me.

I was on the fast track to success. I rose, in my synagogue, to the position of Pharisee, and I learned an excellent trade as a tentmaker.

When I was a young man, a pesky group of people (called Christians) were contaminating the Jewish faith, or at least that is how I thought at the time. I was present when the first of these radicals, Stephen, was "martyred," as several of my friends stoned him to death. Although I did not participate in the stoning, I did hold one of my friend's coats, and I condoned the action. I am not proud of that fact.

I was well respected in the religious community and was good at what I did. What I did well was hunt down Christians and bring them to justice, or what I thought was justice at the time.

It was on one such adventure, to capture Christians that the most bizarre event in my life occurred. I was headed towards Damascus when a massive light from heaven flashed around me, and I fell to the ground. A voice rang out so all in my traveling party could hear: "Saul, Saul, why do you persecute me?"

Let me tell you, if that does not get your attention, nothing will. Oh, I forgot to mention, at the same time, I became blind as a bat. I was scared.

I was then led into the city, where the voice told me I would get additional instructions. For three days, I remained blind and did not eat.

Finally, Ananias, who was one of the Christians, came to me. He laid his hands on me and prayed. The scales fell from my eyes, and I was able to see; at that time I was baptized, and the Holy Spirit came to dwell within me—that same Holy Spirit you have been reading about in this book. It was at this time that many people began to refer to me as Paul rather than Saul.

The Lord had called me to bring his gospel message to the non-Jews, the Gentiles. This mission and ministry was an awesome responsibility, and I was humbled that the Lord chose me.

I am a planner and organizer by nature. Immediately, I began to make travel plans so I could begin my work.

However, it seemed like all of my best-laid plans got messed up somehow. One journey was delayed due to a shipwreck. The devil was working hard to throw my plans of spreading the gospel off track.

Another big plan was to spend a lot of time in Spain doing missionary work, however, I ended up in a Roman jail. That is not how I had planned it.

In Philippians 4:11b-12, I wrote, "I have learned to be content whatever the circumstances. I know what it is like to be in need, and I know what it is to have plenty. I have learned the secret of being content in any and every situation, whether well fed or hungry, whether living in plenty or in want."

Many times, my goals and aspirations were derailed. What should I do? I saw those "circumstances" and problems as an opportunity to see God, and I made the best of them. While I was in jail, I wrote a few letters that you may recognize—letters to Philemon, the Philippians, the Colossians, and the Ephesians. Those letters have been around for about 2,000 years—not bad for making the best out of an apparently bad situation.

In that way, I am like the men at Bibb County. I could not influence whether or not I was in a Roman jail. What I could influence is what I did about it and how I chose to think.

I chose to have a good attitude, an attitude of gratitude and joy for what God had given me. It served me well.

Comments

Paul and the guys at Bibb County were enduring what we would consider a bad situation. In the case of the fellows at Bibb County, they are in that bad situation because they made some bad choices. In Paul's case, he was in prison for some good choices he made. It might not matter what caused the bad situation; the situation exists, and one has to deal with it.

Perhaps you were born with a disability that created what some would consider undue hardship or a bad situation. The causes of "bad" situations are endless—some self-inflicted and some not. In one case, lung cancer may be self-inflicted through years of smoking. In another case, it might be someone was exposed to an environmental hazard. It is still lung cancer, and the individual must deal with it. Is it possible to find joy in this suffering?

Yes, it is possible. Several years ago, as a member of Severna Park United Methodist Church, I served as a Stephen Minister. One of my care receivers was a guy by the name of Hank Spokes. Hank had gotten a diagnosis of lung cancer, and the doctors told him it was inoperable and that he had no more than six months to live. He needed to get his affairs in order. My assignment was to walk with him down this road until it ended.

For at least one evening each week, Hank and I would go get coffee at Starbucks in Annapolis and just talk and pray together. We became great friends, and the six months lasted closer to two years. In that time, we went on fishing trips on the Chesapeake Bay, to lunches, and (of course) to our coffees. One thing I learned is that people who have gotten such a bad diagnosis are hesitant to talk about the issue with family members because they do not want to upset their loved ones. Things that he wanted to discuss, funeral arrangements, were almost taboo. That was part of my role: he could unload on me.

Most of the time, Hank's attitude was so uplifting and cheerful that it was my spirit that got a boost more than his. He certainly reflected the fruit of joy in a horrible situation.

In contrast, I had another care receiver that had gotten a diagnosis of multiple sclerosis. If there is an opposite of joy, that is what that fellow reflected. It was a horrible situation, and I just cannot imagine what he was going through. But the difference between this man and Hank was like night and day. Hank chose joy.

I know the Lord impacted the lives of many around Hank, including co-workers and family, by his reflections of spiritual fruits.

I think Ecclesiastes 8:14-15 has a good message for this fruit: "There is something else meaningless that occurs on earth: the righteous who get what the wicked deserve, and the wicked that get what the righteous deserve. This too, I say, is meaningless. So I commend the enjoyment of life, because there is nothing better for a person under the sun than to eat and drink and be glad. Then joy will accompany them in their toil all the days of the life God has given them under the sun."

Joy is all about your attitude, and again, it is a choice. The thing about joy is that it is contagious. Your joy, or lack of joy, impacts those around you.

I give a workshop on my book, *What I Learned About Leadership From My Dog.* When possible, I bring my dog with me to participate in the workshop. I will very lethargically call Maggie over and give her a few commands. And she will very lethargically obey them. I will then change my attitude, and get excited, and give her the same commands. She gets all excited, and riled up, and executes the commands instantly. The point I am trying to make is my attitude (a choice) impacts the dog's attitude.

As the leader of your organization, you cannot expect others to have a positive attitude if you do not have one.

Discussion Questions:

1. What situations have you experienced that required you to choose to be joyful?
2. What is the best approach when you wake up in a bad mood to go to work? What can you do to reverse that mood?

CHAPTER SIX

Peace

"I CHOOSE PEACE. I will live forgiven. I will forgive so I may live." Max Lucado, *Grace for the Moment.*

Robert Jolly

"I don't love you anymore. I want a divorce."

The words stung. An abusive mom, who he could never please, helped him develop an enormous fear of rejection. Now he had been rejected by the one he loved the most—his lovely wife, the mother of their two children. He was crushed.

I met Robert Jolly at Bibb County Correctional Facility, a state prison in Alabama. Robert and I were part of a team from the Church of the Highlands that was facilitating a study for the inmates. At the time, I had lived in Alabama about a year, after moving from Maryland. When Robert learned this, he chimed in that he had lived in Maryland and had worked for Black & Decker in Towson. Another thing we had in common is Robert is a graduate of the University of Alabama. The story he was telling was one of witnessing to the 150 or so inmates that were in our study group at Bibb.

Robert moved into the guest bedroom, and they filed papers for divorce. What once was an intense love for him had quickly become an intense hate towards the one who had hurt him. He was angry.

Robert and his wife did not speak a word to one another. Eight months went by and not one single word—not "good morning," "get out of my way," or "you forgot to take the trash out"—nothing.

Other things in Robert's life started to become unraveled, such as his job, his health, and other relationships. Life was a mess.

At the time, he was in a Bible study, and he spoke with the facilitator about all of his issues.

The facilitator replied, "You are trying to solve all this yourself. You need to submit and give it to Jesus."

That all sounded good. But these were real issues, tangible issues. This wasn't a go to heaven or hell issue; how could Jesus help?

That evening, Robert knelt on the guest bedroom floor and had a talk with the Lord. He submitted and put these problems in the hands of Jesus. While in prayer, he heard the Lord say to him, "Love her; love your wife."

Robert hated his wife for what she had done to him. He hated her.

Submission is submission. Loving her was going to be a tough choice. To love her also meant he must forgive her.

Robert started leaving his wife love notes each morning—the first letter being something to the effect of "I love you, and I do not want a divorce. I want to raise a family with you."

The next morning, he found that letter wadded up in the trash can. Each morning, he kept writing the letters, and the next day, they were in the trash can. She even wrote him a follow-up note to tell him to stop writing those letters. He continued his love-letter writing.

Then one evening after work, she asked him, "There is an event I want to attend tonight. Would you like to go with me?"

"Well yes!!" he replied.

They started dating again. I heard this story 15 years after that date, and they are still happily married.

Robert chose to forgive. Forgiveness alone does not reconcile a relationship. So somewhere along the line, Robert's wife also did some forgiving, and the two rebuilt trust.

Reconciliation cannot happen without forgiveness.

The Prodigal Son

I am the Prodigal Son. I was not even given a name. I have one older brother, and as law has it, we would eventually divide our father's estate. My father did very well and accumulated much livestock, requiring a lot of hired hands to care for it all.

My brother and I were typical boys, and we had chores. Our father expected us to carry our share of the burden.

I guess I was in my early twenties, when I became restless. As you know, that is not too unusual for young men. I wanted to see new places and be on my own. I did not like being told what to do.

I finally went to my father and demanded my share of the inheritance. I wanted it immediately. I could tell by his reaction that it hurt him, but I really did not care. I was looking out for my interests. As I tell you the story, I relive the feelings of embarrassment of how poorly I behaved and treated my father.

My father sold off a portion of his livestock and paid me in cash. He gave me a hug and wished me well before I left. My older brother did not speak to me he was so angry my departure was met with only a glare on his part.

Up until that point, I had never ventured far away from the main homestead. I began to party. I spent my money on wine, gambling, the best food, and plenty of beautiful women. It did not take me long to go through all of the funds I had.

Now I was broke, and (to add to the problem) there was a famine in the land. I had to go get a job. The jobs I had were not very good—not even enough to support food and lodging. I can recall feeding one of my employer's pigs and wishing I could eat what the pigs were eating.

It finally dawned on me—my Dad's hired hands had it much better. If my Dad would only hire me as a worker, I would have a place to sleep and plenty of food to eat. I decided to swallow my pride and head home to ask forgiveness and for a job.

On the long journey back home, I ran over what I would say a hundred times in my mind—how I would sell my Dad on the idea of me working for him. I had left on a very bad note. I would not blame my Dad at all if he even refused to talk with me, much less hire me.

After several days of travel, I finally topped the last hill and could see the sprawling homestead below. I had mixed emotions. It was wonderful to be home, but anxiety was the main emotion—how would everyone react?

After I was about one-third down the hill, I saw a scurrying of activity and several men beginning to run in my direction. My anxiety increased.

At about 100 yards, I was able to recognize my Dad was running out front. He held up his robe so he could run as fast as possible. He was headed directly for me as fast as he could.

What happened next I will never be able to fully explain; as I started to speak, my Dad embraced me, kissed my cheek time and time again, and would not let me apologize. He kept telling me how much he had missed me and how much he loved me. By now, the other men had caught up. My father turned to them and exclaimed, "My son has returned. Go get the fattest calf, and let's have a celebration."

The party was wonderful, and the celebration went well into the night.

There was only one sour note—my older brother would not attend. Later, I learned that he was very upset with Dad for welcoming me back. He was angry that a party was given for me and that Dad never threw a party for him. I understand, and I am not mad at my brother. I pray that one day, he will choose to forgive me. If only my brother would reflect the fruit of peace like Robert Jolly.

Comments

How does forgiveness work in a leadership setting? One of the old foundations I have always heard is that the best indicator of future behavior is past behavior. What does "forgiving" past behaviors/offensives look like?

As individuals, we are called to forgive those who have offended us. It is not an option. We are told in numerous ways that we are forgiven as we forgive.

Many times, we have the wrong idea of forgiveness. Forgiveness does not mean minimizing the offense or forgetting what happened. It also does not mean the relationship must be restored. It takes two to restore a relationship but only one for forgiveness.

In the situation of the prodigal son, the youngest son squandered his inheritance. The longterm consequence to this is he squandered his share—what is remaining belongs to the older brother. The father loved him and forgave him, but the fact remains that the wealth was gone as far as the younger brother was concerned. So perhaps the element of the impact on others is something that must be considered.

If someone has had an on-again, off-again problem with drugs or alcohol, what does forgiveness look like? Would you hire this person as a fork truck driver for your plant? No, you wouldn't because that would adversely affect the safety of others. Not getting the job is a consequence of the behavior.

Not every situation is one where people's safety is at risk. Many employers will not consider hiring people who have served time in prison. Perhaps there is an area where we could explore some forgiveness in the workplace, assuming the offender is now on a good path.

Perhaps peace/forgiveness also has something to do with trust. Do you trust those working for you? I do not mean whether or not they are stealing or lying—do you trust them to do their job without you micromanaging them and exerting excessive control?

I think we can re-word the question to say, "Do I believe you know what you are doing?" If the answer to that question is "yes," then let them do their job with no interference from you. If the answer is "no," then the next question for yourself should be, "What will it take for me to say 'yes' to the question?"

Will it require a certain certification, passing a test, etc.? Do I need to witness your proficiency? You need to do whatever it takes to answer the question.

Discussion

1. What does forgiveness look like in the workplace?
2. How do you balance your responsibility to the whole organization with the forgiveness of individuals?
3. Do you need to forgive anyone in your sphere of influence?
4. What roles do education and training play in forgiveness and trust in the workplace?

CHAPTER SEVEN

Patience

"I CHOOSE PATIENCE. I will overlook the inconveniences of the world. Instead of cursing the one who takes my place, I'll invite him to do so. Rather than complain that the wait is too long, I will thank God for a moment to pray. Instead of clenching my fist at new assignments, I will face them with courage." Max Lucado, *Grace for the Moment.*

Linda Covington

One winter morning, our phone rang at 2:00 AM. This was not too much of a problem, as my wife Linda stays up to about 3:00, and I get up around 5:00.

Linda answered the phone, and the caller asked to speak to me (remember, it's 2:00 AM—like in the morning). She told them that I was asleep. The caller said, "okay," and started to hang up.

Linda is still pretty sharp at 2:00 AM and said, "Hold on just a second. You call here at 2:00 in the morning, asking for my husband, and you are just going to hang up? Who are you?"

Right away, that exchange should have been a warning sign to ignore the whole thing. The caller was a lady from our alarm company. The motion detector in the company break room had been activated, and they called the police. She wanted to know if we wanted to meet the police at the office. Linda woke me up, and in a moment of temporary insanity, we decided that both of us should go to the office and meet up with the police.

Linda is normally insulated from the massive chaos caused by my daughter and me. We have been married since 1972, and there always seems to be some sort of oddball thing going on. Most times, Linda is a casual observer and has just enjoyed the ongoing sitcom. This time, she had injected herself into the fray.

I threw on some clothes, and off we went. We forgot our cell phone and the closest thing we had to a weapon, Maggie, our one-and-a-half-year-old German Shepherd, who is an expert at chasing tennis balls and eating from the cat's litter box.

Our office is less than four miles away, so we were there in a flash—but there were no police. We drove around to the back of the building and noticed that the lights in the break room were on. Very suspicious (I later remembered that our admin staff had left early that day and had given me one measly task to do—be sure and shut off the lights in the breakroom before you leave—oops). However, at the moment, we were convinced we had a bad guy in the break room enjoying a snack at 2:30 AM.

Linda nixed the idea of me going in the building with no weapon—the robbers would surely shoot me, abduct her, and we would have a big mess on our hands. We decided to rush back to the house to get the cell phone and our 85-pound bundle of "cat-poop eating terror."

We arrived back at the building, prepared for this emergency. Maggie was convinced that Linda and I have lost our mind, but (from her perspective) all car rides, except those that end at the vet, are a good deal. She was ready for some fun. Maggie and I went to "sweep" the building while Linda waited in the car. Even though we accomplished our tasks in less than five minutes, Linda was getting impatient, as it is 22 degrees outside, and I had the car keys. She was ruing the decision to join Maggie and me on this excursion. It would have been toastier to stay at home and prepare for bedtime.

I reset the alarm, and having ensured our facility was void of evil bad guys, Maggie and I proudly went back to the car.

Linda had her hands out; "What do you want?" I asked. "The car keys—I'm freezing," she said. I dug around in my pockets, and the fact quickly set in that I have locked the office keys and car keys in the building. We were in deep poop—very chilly deep poop.

Evidently, the humor of the situation hit me, and I must have had a slight grin on my face. Linda's icy comment was, "THIS IS NOT FUNNY! **YOU** BETTER THINK OF SOMETHING QUICK!"

From my limited knowledge of wife behavior, I suspected that she was not pleased with me.

It was now about 2:45—still in the morning. It was also 22 degrees, and the car was getting cold. I figured that since we did not run into the police, I would give them a buzz, so I called 911. I explained to the dispatcher that we were supposed to meet the police at our office. She told me that they had already been there and did not see any problem. I told her our predicament and asked if they could make another swing by the office and give us a lift home. She put me on hold while she checked.

After a while, she came back on the line and said something to the effect of, "Sir, we do not get cats out of trees or rescue idiots who lock themselves outside in 22-degree weather. We catch bad guys. I suggest you call a cab. I certainly hope you were smart enough not to bring your poor wife with you." Aaah!

The thought of walking home crossed my mind, as it is only 3.5 miles, and we could make it in about an hour. Linda did not think that was a good idea. Her response to that suggestion cannot be printed. After giving it some thought, I did not think it was such a hot idea either. Walking down a lonely trail at night (with a wife who was considering murder) just sounds stupid.

I called a cab company in Annapolis, which is about 10 miles from our office. The dispatcher said they were "busy."

"Busy??" I said, "How is it possible that you are busy? It is 3:00 in the morning!"

He was sticking to his story and said something about the bars just closing. I guess if I would have told him we were drunk, he would have come. Anyway, he gave us the number of another cab company, whose dispatcher that said they would have a cab there in 20 minutes.

Linda's humor was now starting to improve. It may be she was going into hypothermia, which I understand tends to calm you. Our next challenge was to sneak Maggie into the back seat of the cab, as leaving her in the car was not going to be an option. Leaving me in the car was an option but not the dog. Fortunately, we had a canine-loving cab driver who also waited until he was certain that we had also not locked ourselves out of our house. He did suggest that we get Maggie some doggie breath mints (if he only knew). The net result of the night was I lost nearly two hours of sleep, Linda was a tad late getting to bed, and we have this neat story to tell, which has amused our neighbors.

When I talk to my friends about this book and tell them that Linda is my example for patience, they laugh out loud—to my face they laugh out loud.

"She has been married to you for over four decades. She is the patron saint of patience" is a typical response.

Mary

My name is Mary. I have had a very interesting life to say the least. The fruit of patience has served me well in enabling me to maintain a healthy outlook.

I was probably about thirteen years old when I noticed a handsome young man, Joseph, in our town, Nazareth, which was in Galilee. He was several years older than me, and he was learning to become a carpenter. Every opportunity I got, I would try and catch his eye. He later told me that he had his eye on me also.

I was ecstatic when I learned that our families had arranged for us to be married. I was so proud to be engaged to him and was looking forward to raising a family together.

The typical wedding plans were being made, and there was much excitement among our families.

Then everything changed. I was in prayer and meditation one evening when the angel, Gabriel, spoke to me, saying, "Hail, O favored one, the Lord is with you." (Luke 1:28b)

Of course I was shocked, but I was also confused as to what that meant. Gabriel went on to assure me and told me not to be afraid. He said that I would conceive and bear a son and that I shall name him Jesus.

I can now look back upon the time and chuckle a bit, but I was terrified then. Thousands of questions went through my mind— "How could this happen?" "What am I going to tell Joseph and my family?"

Gabriel also told me that my kinswoman, Elizabeth, who was very old and past childbearing age, was also having a child and was already in her sixth month. That seemed impossible, but it was true. This was a miracle from God, just like Sara becoming pregnant at an old age.

To this day, I do not understand the attitude of my wonderful husband, Joseph. He very well could have divorced me, but he did not. He just loved me. I think that angel may have also paid him a visit or two.

The disruptions seemed to never stop. Not long before I was due to deliver, Caesar Augustus declared that a census needed to be taken. Joseph's family was originally from Bethlehem, which was all the way in Judea. If Linda thought sitting in a cold car was bad, she should try riding several days on a donkey, days before delivering a child.

When we finally got to Bethlehem, there were no rooms, as there were so many people in town because of the census. We ended up staying in an animal stall. However, I had no trouble, and my baby was beautiful. Gabriel had told me how special this child was. We had all sorts of visitors and people wanting to praise God for this moment.

I was ready for Joseph, our new baby, and me to head home. However, yet another disruption—we were warned that Herod was looking for the new king and that we were to go to Egypt and wait until we got word to return home.

I was not even fifteen years old and had already experienced more excitement than most women experience in a lifetime.

Joseph and I were blessed with several other children, and for the most part, we lived a normal life.

As Jesus grew older, Joseph and I were constantly reminded by events how special he was—the Son of God. Our entire family was visiting Jerusalem one year during Passover, and we were headed home. After we had been on our journey for two days, we noticed that Jesus was no longer with us. You parents know the feeling of fright when one of your children is missing. We searched all over and found him teaching and asking questions at the temple. I suspect that Jesus himself began to understand his special calling at that time.

When my son began his ministry, more stress came to our family. Some of his siblings thought he had lost his mind, and that caused friction.

You know the rest of my story and can just imagine the emotions of having your son executed before your eyes, then three days later, the elation of learning he was alive.

I hope that some of the examples of my life can reflect the fruit of patience for you.

Comments

How do we act when our well-laid plans get knocked off track by some unplanned event? It could be a flat tire, a traffic delay, or a nasty case of the flu. Do we lose our temper and lash out in anger or retreat into a corner and fret?

Are we able to adjust to what happened and reprogram our thinking to focus on the new situation?

Whereas the fruit of Joy is being able to find peace and happiness in just about any situation, patience is the ability to adapt in an appropriate and kind manner to things that pop up unexpectedly.

Unexpected surprises happen. The ability to calmly address the numerous issues that come your way in a manner that does not hurt people but evokes confidence is critically important.

Discussion

1. What was the most recent disruption you have experienced?
2. What would you have done differently, if anything?
3. What does the Holy Spirit do to help you adjust?
4. What effect does a leader's patience have in the workplace?
5. Without using the word "impatience," describe the opposite of patience. What does it look like?

CHAPTER EIGHT

Kindness

"I CHOOSE KINDNESS. I will be kind to the poor, for they are alone. Kind to the rich, for they are afraid. And kind to the unkind, for such is how God has treated me." Max Lucado, *Grace for the Moment.*

Gene Cuzzart

It was 2:30 AM. All was quiet as the 40 souls slept in a warm environment. It was February in Severna Park, Maryland, and the wind-chill factor outside would cut right to your bones. For a variety of reasons, these 40 people were homeless.

To maintain safety, someone needed to be awake and alert in case of an emergency. Gene had taken a week of vacation to serve these people. Instead of going to Florida to bask in the sun, he chose to stay near home and sit alone in the fellowship hall of the church—a book and some coffee to keep him occupied, away from family and friends. What a neat and unselfish way to spend one's vacation time!

My wife, Linda, and I first met Gene and his lovely wife, Sandy, on a church mission trip to Rosebud Indian Reservation in South Dakota. Again, Gene was using his vacation time to serve others. We instantly became friends.

In addition to being a really neat guy, Gene is a University of Alabama football fan. He is especially fond of Barry Krauss, who was an All-American linebacker at Alabama and played for the Baltimore Colts.

I had met Barry through some business connections and asked him if he would have dinner with Gene and me when we were down to Tuscaloosa for a game. Barry is one of the nicest fellows you are going to meet, and he quickly agreed to the dinner. Barry brought his fiancé, and it was just a delightful evening, one Gene will never forget.

Later, Gene and I went on several mission trips without our wives, and we discovered that both of us were "morning people." Whether it was East Tennessee or the jungles of Costa Rica, we were always the first up and had the coffee hot for everyone else. Sometimes, those traveling with us did not share our enthusiasm for early morning discussions.

On a mission trip to Tennessee, Gene and I were drinking our coffee and discussing some of the finer points out of the book of Nehemiah. It was probably about 5:15 in the morning, and we were propped on the front porch of a cabin, directly in front of the room where our friend and head of our group, Mel Merritt, was trying to sleep. Mel was quite vocal in letting us know his displeasure, and he still harasses us about the early morning discussion. If given the opportunity, Gene and I would do it again just to mess with Mel.

I asked Gene how he became involved in this type of work for the Lord. He said it started off as a dare from Sandy. She challenged him to go on a trip to Guatemala. He loved the trip and went on a second mission trip to Guatemala. It was on that second trip that he felt the Holy Spirit speaking to him and saying, "You are doing what you are supposed to be doing."

When talking about what he has to offer, he told me, "I do not have a lot of money. But I have six weeks of vacation."

Gene was also kind to his friends, including me. He was one of my sponsors on my "Walk To Emmaus."

He has a talent and a passion for working with youth, so in recent years, that is where he has placed his focus, serving with the Appalachian Service Project and other youth-related ministries.

The Good Samaritan

I am a businessman from Samaria. One afternoon, I was traveling from Jerusalem to Jericho. The trip was going to be several days, so I brought my donkey along to carry my gear. It was a long, winding road down the mountain from Jerusalem. About halfway down the mountain, I spotted a man lying on the other side of the road. I first started to pass by, but something told me to stop; that little voice that sometimes taps you on the shoulder and tells you to do something was nudging me.

The poor man was in terrible shape. It looked as though he had been attacked by robbers. Not only were all of his possessions gone, but he had been badly beaten.

I spent some time cleaning and bandaging his wounds and trying to get him to drink some water. He was in no condition to leave on the side of the road, so I helped him up onto my donkey. I had noticed an inn several miles back, so I headed back up the mountain.

I helped him inside and paid for a room for several nights. The innkeeper helped me get him to his room and tucked into a comfortable bed. Before I left, I told the innkeeper that I would stop back by his inn on my way home, and if there were any additional charges, I would pay for them then. He was a very nice man and trusted me to return. Many people in this region do not like Samaritans. The hatred had to do with some political problems between regions hundreds of years ago. I was always made to feel like a second-class citizen because I was Samaritan.

Centuries have gone by, and I now see that I am referred to as "The Good Samaritan." I wish I had known that back in my youth, as I would have made sure my wife and boss were aware of my elevated status—ha.

I learned that before I ventured upon the scene, several religious leaders had come by and actually made an effort to go to the opposite side of the road to avoid the injured man. My guess is they did not have that little voice helping them make good and kind decisions.

Comments

Kindness seems to always involve someone going out of one's way to do something. A person has a routine, and they stop that routine to do something for someone else.

From time to time, we all run across panhandlers or homeless people. How would you judge your attitude towards such people? Mine is a mixed bag. Sometimes, I do a good job. That might not mean giving them money, as I might not have any money with me. What it does mean is treating them with love and respect. Perhaps it is making eye contact and earnestly asking how they are doing. It also means helping them in any manner possible, within your ability.

Kindness is all about making people feel special and unique. They are not just another number, or employee, or face in the crowd. Take time to be kind to your people—talk with them, engage in small and large acts of kindness. Take time to learn their hobbies and their spouse's name. Ask how they are doing. Let your people know they are special. The impact goes well beyond your company's performance.

Discussion

1. What would be an example of someone being kind to a rich person?
2. When have you gone out of your way/been inconvenienced for someone else?
3. What role does the Holy Spirit play in these inconveniences?

CHAPTER NINE

Goodness

"I CHOOSE GOODNESS. I will go without a dollar before I take a dishonest one. I will be overlooked before I will boast. I will confess before I accuse." Max Lucado, *Grace for the Moment.*

Leroy McAbee

We were in San Destin, Florida for a University of Alabama College of Engineering board meeting. Most members of the board were there because they were extremely successful. I was there because I happened to be the chairman of the chemical engineering advisory board. They have since changed the rules, but they grandfathered me in. I was lucky.

Many of the members played golf, so after our meeting that ended at lunch, most went to hit the links. I decided not to put my fellow board members in danger (plus embarrass myself), so I rented a bike.

San Destin is a beautiful location. Our meeting was on the Gulf of Mexico side of a major highway. To get to the other part of the San Destin community, you went through a tunnel under the highway. It was a great bike ride—the Gulf on one side and beautiful homes, ponds, and wooded areas on the other. I rode for several hours and was headed back.

As I peddled past a pond on my right, I saw what looked to be a panther. *Impossible*, I thought.

Sure enough, there was a large panther on the other side of the pond, giving me one of those looks as if I might be on his menu. I couldn't believe it. I stopped the next biker and asked him to tell me what he saw on the other side of the pond. I cannot print his exact words, but it was something to the effect of "Holy cow! There is a panther over there."

After we had regained our composure, the seriousness of the issue took center stage. This was a residential area with kids, pets, joggers, and (of course) bike riders all around. Mr. Panther did not need to be one of the San Destin neighbors. I rode my bike to the guard shack and explained what I had seen. The guard looked at me like I had three heads and was subtly trying to smell the tequila on my breath. I was getting nowhere with the guard.

I finally said, "Look mister, this time tomorrow, I will be on a plane back to Maryland. However, you and Mr. Panther are going to be right here coexisting with one another. I suggest you call a forest ranger or start packing a gun."

When I got back to our hotel and relayed my story to my fellow board members, they also were accusing me of beginning happy hour way too early. That was my early introduction to our prestigious board. I was deemed sane enough to continue—thank heavens. I have met some wonderful people who have become good friends with me, and one of them is Leroy McAbee. Let me tell you about Leroy.

"John, we need to take care of young people and old people. All of us in the middle need to do our part," Leroy said.

My friend, Leroy McAbee, was 85 years old when we were in his office in Tuscaloosa, Alabama, and he was explaining his ideas on helping people. I was not going to suggest to Leroy that some folks might think 85 is a little long in the tooth, as I was not about to wear out my welcome.

Every square inch of the walls in Leroy's office had something hanging. His office wall probably did a good job of reflecting his life to date. There was a picture of him with his Korean War buddies; there were Boy Scout Council Awards for his philanthropy; there were several horse collars (probably reminding him of some of his rural roots); and there was an old rifle.

"John, let me tell you about that rifle. I had an employee years ago that claimed he hurt his back on the job, drew Workman's Compensation (money from the company), then quit work. Several years later, he shows up in my office with that rifle. He wanted me to forgive him. I asked him what he did, and he told me that he had cheated me and had stolen money. He said that two years earlier, he had fallen out of a tree while hunting, hurt his back, and then claimed he had hurt it on the job. He said he did not have the money to pay me back, but he wanted to give me the rifle in return for my forgiveness. I told him, 'Sure.'"

That is one of the more bizarre stories I have heard about a memento on a wall and may give you some insight into Leroy.

I completed explaining to Leroy what I was attempting to do with this book, and it seemed to meet his satisfaction, at least well enough to continue the discussion.

He was born in Centre, Alabama, a rural community, and raised in Rome and Savannah, Georgia during the Great Depression and World War ll. He considered going to college, but the war had displaced most of the American men as soldiers, so there were not enough teachers. He did not feel his math and science skills were good enough to get into the University of Alabama—the school of his dreams.

By the time he grew up, America was at war in Korea. Leroy joined the Army and served as a combat engineer. His father had encouraged him to learn a trade, so he became a pipe fitter and was good enough to become a young foreman on many jobs. He was traveling around the country, making plenty of money in the pipe-fitting business, when his sister, Doris, called about the urgency of enrolling at Alabama before his GI bill ran out. Leroy was still convinced he would not get in. Doris, who was already enrolled at Alabama, had more confidence in her older brother than he did and convinced him to leave Idaho and come to Tuscaloosa. Doris provided a last enticement when she told him there were plenty of pretty girls on campus. Leroy enrolled at Alabama in 1955 to study Mechanical Engineering.

Leroy worked his way through school to supplement the GI Bill, and he graduated in 1961. He also found one of those pretty girls, married her, and immediately went to work for an engineering construction firm located in Greenville, SC. After a year of lots of travel and being away from his wife, Babe, and young child, he decided to quit the firm, move to Tuscaloosa, and go into business himself. He founded McAbee Construction in 1962— just one year after he graduated from college.

Penny Ford, the pastor at Trinity United Methodist in Tuscaloosa, Alabama, wanted to tell me a Leroy McAbee story once she learned that I knew him. She was at the airport with her aging dad and ran into Leroy. Penny's father was a disabled veteran and was confined to a wheelchair. It was a casual conversation, and somehow, the topic got around to the need for a wheelchair ramp at the family home so her dad could attend functions there. It was a comment made in passing.

Several weeks later, Penny heard a commotion outside and went to investigate. There, to her surprise, was a crew from McAbee Construction building a wheelchair ramp.

In my meeting with Leroy, I started to tell him the story, and as soon as I mentioned Penny Ford's name, he smiled and said, "Her dad is my friend."

In 2011, a tornado hit Tuscaloosa and devastated the community. When one of my neighbors found out I was an engineering graduate of Alabama, she asked me if I knew Leroy. I told her I did. She went on to rave about how a large tree was on their home, and how she had mentioned it to a friend of hers who happened to work at McAbee. The next day, she heard a chainsaw and went out to find a crew from McAbee Construction removing the tree.

These are two small stories that (of course) got no press or public recognition. There must be thousands more just like these two.

Leroy's many good causes that are a matter of public record include Boy Scouts of America, Druid City Hospital, United Way of Tuscaloosa County, University of Alabama, and McAbee Senior Citizens Center.

Remember: young people and old people, and (of course) Leroy joins those of us in the middle.

Joseph

My name is Joseph. I did not start out reflecting the fruit of goodness, as I was pretty much about myself. Some of that may have come from my father, Jacob, doting on me. I was his youngest son at the time and also the son of Rachael, the woman my father loved the most. Dad went out of his way to spoil me.

He had a beautiful and colorful robe made for me. The robe was like none other. I wore that robe everywhere, which I later learned was hurtful to my brothers and made them angry. Dad did not make any of them a fine robe. Again, I really did not pay too much attention to their feelings.

I made matters worse by telling my brothers and my parents about dreams that I had where I ended up being in great power over all of my brothers and my parents. Obviously, humility was not a characteristic I had as a young man.

My father also spoiled me with regard to sharing the household chores. While my brothers were out caring for the sheep, I was normally given some small task that would keep me around the house.

One day, my Dad asked me to go to the field and check on my brothers. I donned my robe, and off I went.

From a distance, my brothers saw me coming, and they plotted a way to kill me. I guess I had made them a lot more mad than I thought. Lucky for me, one of my brothers, Reuben, came up with a scheme to save me.

When I approached, they grabbed me, ripped off my beautiful robe, beat me, and then threw me into a cistern. I was shocked and scared. I did not know their plan—were they going to kill me? How could my own brothers do this to me? I longed to be home with my father.

Several days went by, and a caravan passed by on its way to Egypt. My brothers sold me to those Ishmaelites. Later, I learned my brothers killed an animal, soaked my robe in its blood, and told my father that I had been killed by a wild animal.

On the journey to Egypt, I had plenty of time to think—and to worry. This was a humbling, humiliating, and scary experience. What was in store for me?

I was sold to Potiphar, who was an officer of Pharaoh. The Lord blessed everything that I did, and soon, Potiphar put me in charge of nearly all of his estate. It was while working for Potiphar that one of my trials occurred.

As a young man, many told me that I was handsome and attractive to the ladies. Potiphar's wife seemed to have eyes for me and tried numerous times to entice me to sleep with her. I always rejected her advances. One day, she grabbed me, and I tore away. She screamed as if I had been the aggressor. The other servants came, and she told everyone that I had attempted to rape her. I guess I was fortunate to avoid execution. However, I ended up in prison. I never threw Potiphar's wife under the bus and told on her. I kept her advances and lies to myself.

While in prison, I met some fellows that were having a hard time interpreting their dreams. One was a butler and the other a baker. I accurately interpreted their dreams, which included the butler being released. I asked him to remember me when he left prison.

The butler promptly forgot me when he got his release. However, a time came when Pharaoh had a dream that no one could interpret. Pharaoh was concerned that he could not find an answer. Finally, the butler remembered me, and I was released from prison.

I told Pharaoh that his dream had to do with a drought coming upon his land after seven years of plentiful harvest. What needed to happen is someone had to manage the grain in a manner that they stored excess during the good years so they would have plenty during the famine. Pharaoh chose me for that job.

The job required that I be disciplined and fair. I did such a good job that eventually there was no one in Egypt, except Pharaoh, who had more power.

When the famine arrived, all of the surrounding countries looked to Egypt for food. This included my family in Canaan. My brothers, the same ones that sold me into slavery, came to me, wanting to purchase grain. They did not recognize me, and initially, I did not make my identity known. I tricked them to get them to bring my younger brother, Benjamin, to see me. Eventually, my brothers went back home to bring my father, Jacob, to Egypt, and our family was reunited. My brothers were afraid when they realized who I was and how much power was in my hands. However, I took a page from the book of the prodigal son's father—I forgave them. I did get in one final dig—*"You intended to harm me, but God intended it for good to accomplish what is now being done, the saving of many lives." Genesis 50:20*

Comments

Sue Engle, who is the Resource Director in the Memphis Conference of the United Methodist Church, wrote a week's worth of devotionals for the 2016 edition of *Disciplines*. The title she gave her week was "Transforming Mercies." Here is a quote from her devotional that can be found on page 256:

"If we have more than what we need, might we share it with others? Generosity grows our faith. Blessing others when we have been blessed extends the transforming mercies from us to others. Why does God choose to limit Himself in meeting needs through partnership with us? Free will presents a serious risk in that we often choose poorly. Transforming mercies give us an opportunity to make better choices each day."

The reason I selected Leroy McAbee for this section is it is easy to see the impact of what he has done because of the magnitude.

I think Luke 16:10-11 is an appropriate scripture to ponder in this section: "Whoever can be trusted with very little can also be trusted with much, and whoever is dishonest with very little will also be dishonest with much. So if you have not been trustworthy in handling worldly wealth, who will trust you with true riches?"

Talking about prospering by being a Christian is a slippery slope. Again, the Holy Spirit is following me around, as our pastor did a sermon on the issue of prosperity. This conversation on prosperity is directly from his sermon notes.

It is horrible for when a TV evangelist promises people who send money will have nice things happen to them, such as becoming wealthy. That is simply wrong, and people who preach that sort of nonsense are misguided.

So, what does it actually mean then? The Hebrew word for "prosper" is actually closer to the meaning of "to push forward." God is pushing you forward to do more. Biblical prosperity is having more than you need so you can make a difference in the lives of others. God blesses people so they will be a blessing to others. The more God blesses us, the more He expects us to bless others. There is an old saying "for he who has plenty; plenty will be expected," or something to that effect. God does not want people to feel guilty for what they have; He just wants them to be responsible.

1 Timothy 6:17-19 is excellent: "Command those who are rich in this present world not to be arrogant nor to put their hope in wealth, which is so uncertain, but to put their hope in God, who richly provides us with everything for our enjoyment. Command them to do good, to be rich in good deeds, and to be generous and willing to share. In this way they will lay up treasure for themselves as a firm foundation for the coming age, so that they may take hold of the life that is truly life."

Another wonderful example is John Wesley, the founder of what is now the United Methodist Church. Wesley lived long enough to realize financial gain from all of his books and writings. Wesley kept enough money for food and shelter and gave the rest of his revenue to the poor.

All of the fruits of the spirit are choices. Leroy has chosen to align his behavior with the Holy Spirt and has let the Spirit work through him to bless others.

When I was reading Everybody Matters, Bob Chapman took me back to a memory I had running my own business. The economy had tanked, and our business really took a hit with regard to new orders and ongoing business. I was faced with having a serious layoff, something we had never done before.

Being laid off can be devastating to a family. Unfortunately, downsizing, right-sizing, re-engineering, etc., has almost become commonplace over the last several decades. What we chose to do is give everyone a pay cut, even those in the part of the business that was still doing well. For that time, it saved many jobs, and only one person objected. That one person eventually left, and that was probably a good thing.

Discussion

1. What friend of yours demonstrates the fruit of Goodness?
2. You are having cash flow problems. A customer accidently overpays you by $2000. It is a large job, and they will never notice. What do you do? What are the consequences either way?
3. In what way do you currently use your blessings to bless others?
4. When Jesus asks you upon your death, "What have you done with what I have given you?" how will you feel?

CHAPTER TEN

Faithfulness

"I CHOOSE FAITHFULNESS. Today I will keep my promise. My debtors will not regret their trust. My associates will not question my word. My wife will not question my love. And my children will never fear that their father will not come home." Max Lucado, *Grace for the Moment*.

Leigh Covington

We were living in Chattanooga, Tennessee at the time. Leigh and I were going on one of those Daddy/Daughter walks. She was six or seven at the time and still enjoyed holding my hand as we strolled and discussed deep philosophical things.

There was a little girl who lived across the street from us and had been bullying Leigh. Leigh was much more athletic and could clean the girl's clock if pressed. As her dad, I was tired of seeing her bullied and wanted justice to prevail.

"Why don't you just hit her back?" I suggested.

She replied, "Because that is not what Jesus would want me to do."

Hmm—who is the teacher here?

You will have to excuse me some on this fruit, as some "daddy pride" is bound to ooze out.

Leigh graduated from the University of Alabama in four years. That was quite an accomplishment considering she changed her major at least three times, worked while in school, and had a nasty bout with learning she was a type 1 diabetic. After graduation, she was off to the Dallas, Texas area to be a restaurant manager for Johnny Carinos. Most of her employees were Hispanic, which was going to be an opportunity for old dad to have an "I told you so" moment.

When Leigh was in high school, I strongly advised her to take Spanish. My thought process was we are getting a lot of immigrants from Spanish speaking countries, and it would be an excellent idea to be able to speak their language. In typical Leigh fashion, she took French instead. To me, French appeared to be about as useless as Latin.

During our first visit to Dallas to visit Leigh, she was telling us that when her employees got mad at her, they would pretend to not be able to understand English. It was the perfect opportunity for me to pounce;

"So, Leigh, I think I recall suggesting to you years ago that you take Spanish, and you chose to take French. Any regrets?"

Leigh replied, "Oh Dad, French works just fine. Whenever they pretend like they do not understand, I just start speaking French to them. They do not like it when they cannot understand what I am saying. So I cut a deal with them—they speak English, and I will speak English."

Oh well, so much for daddy wisdom.

Leigh made the decision to move back to Alabama. The employees at Carinos gave her a farewell party. It was very emotional. Somehow, this young woman had touched these employees so much with her love and loyalty that it was a traumatic event for them to lose her. One of the cooks was so upset she would not come out of the ladies room where she was weeping. One of the young waiters brought her a CD of Spanish love songs. I have been around a lot of transitions, and this one appeared to be somewhat over the top.

The last restaurant she managed was one in Birmingham. When she left that facility to come to work for Chesapeake, I observed the same response from her crew. One lady came over to Leigh's apartment and gave her rosary beads. She brought one of the young Hispanic men with her, who could also speak good English, so he could translate her words of love to Leigh.

Leigh was faithful to her employees.

Some of her restaurant stories are really funny. One of my favorites had to do with catching their dumpster on fire when she was managing a Chili's restaurant.

Several of her employees were smoking outside and tossed their butts in the dumpster. Well, they were not totally out, and the dumpster went up in flames. The fire department was called, and they put the fire out. To be on the safe side, they stuffed a rag in the drain hole and filled the dumpster with water to ensure it would not reignite.

As they left, one of the firemen told Leigh, "Now do not forget to pull out that rag before you leave."

The next morning, Leigh heard an awful sound of a straining motor, coming from the outside of her office where the dumpster was located. Of course, she had forgotten to take out the rag, and the truck was in the process of hoisting a dumpster full of garbage and water. Well, all of the water and garbage come crashing into the truck. The driver had his window down, so he was now soaked with this foul-smelling concoction.

The next thing Leigh heard was a really angry garbage truck driver beating on the back door of her restaurant, wanting to talk to the person in charge.

I asked Leigh what the fellow had to say.

She answered, "Dad, do I just look stupid? I was not about to answer that door."

I used to say she got that bizarre behavior from her mother. However, note that her mother was listed as an example of the fruit of "patience."

My daughter is an attractive lady, and young men took notice, including one fellow from the Dallas area who wanted to date her. However, she had a steady boyfriend she had met in college, and although she was tempted, she remained faithful to her Tuscaloosa boyfriend. Unfortunately, the boy did not exhibit the fruit of faithfulness, and hence, the relationship did not work out.

Recently, she reached out to a lady her age, who had once been a friend. The girl had betrayed Leigh's friendship numerous times. The vast majority of people I know would have written off this girl long ago. Through Facebook, Leigh discovered the girl was having some problems and was looking for some relief; hence, Leigh reached out. Will they become best buddies again? I doubt it. However, she was faithful to this girl even though the faithfulness was not returned.

I could list at least 100 examples of Leigh's loyalty and faithfulness to people, pets, and organizations.

Leigh is one you can trust to be there when needed.

Ruth

My name is Ruth, and I am from Moab. I became the great-grandmother of the greatest king of Israel, King David, who is in the genealogy of Jesus Christ. My story is one of loyalty.

As a young girl, I fell in love with a Hebrew man whose family was foreign in our land. My father-in-law was Elimelech, and my mother-in-law was Naomi. They had two sons. I married one, and another son married Orpah, who was also a Moabite woman.

Not too long after we were married, Elimelech died, leaving Naomi with just her two sons, Orpah, and me. About ten years later, my husband and his brother died, leaving just us three women to fend for ourselves.

Naomi had always missed her home in Judah and had learned that there was now plenty of food there. She decided to return. When she began her journey, Orpah and I followed her. Naomi felt it was best for us to stay in our home country of Moab. However, we followed despite her objections. It was a constant argument on the trip. Finally, Orpah relented and decided to say farewell to Naomi and me and to stay in Moab.

Naomi continued to nag me about staying in Moab. We finally had one last argument on the subject. I told her that I loved her and that I would die where she planned on dying. She never nagged me on the topic again.

Once we were in Judah, my loyalty and devotion to Naomi caught the eye of Boaz, one of her relatives and a wealthy man. Boaz was a kind man. We fell in love and were married. Our first son was Obed, who I dedicated to my mother-in-law, Naomi. Obed was the father of Jesse, who was the father of David (who became king of Israel).

Like Leigh, you can count on me to be there when needed.

Comments

Faithfulness means ignoring self-gratification and self-benefit and remaining loyal no matter what. The vast majority of privately owned companies I have worked with over the years are like that. I have not seen the same loyalty demonstrated by publically held companies as they are more loyal to their stockholders, and perhaps that is the nature of the beast.

We did a lot of work for the furniture industry in their heyday. Stanley Furniture was the first large company and then Bassett Furniture. Both companies had multiple plants. Many of the workers in these plants would classify as "lower middle class," and these jobs were a source of pride and pretty good income, along with company benefits. Around the year 2000, many of these companies began looking to China for some of their product, especially for some of the more ornate designs that required a lot of hand carving.

The Chinese, as business people, cannot be trusted. I hate making blanket statements like this, but they have proved it time and time again by "knocking off" products and pirating. In the furniture industry, the Chinese factories began offering their product for sale to the U.S. companies for less than the Chinese manufacturing cost. As you know—that is illegal. It was shown to be illegal but the executives of the major companies overlooked this because they could make more money by shutting their own factories down and by purchasing the low priced Chinese goods.

This entire scheme was exposed in the book, *Factory Man*, by Beth Macy. In my nearly 30 years of being in business, I do not know if I have ever been as angry. By the way, being angry at an injustice is a good thing.

That is what faithfulness does not look like.

Being faithful to people also means not gossiping behind their back. It means assuming the best and not letting negativity creep in.

Your employees want to know that you have their best interests at heart and that you want them to be successful and to accomplish their goals.

Discussion

1. You work for an accounting firm. Business has been slow for the last four years. However, your employer has not cut your hours nor even mentioned laying you off. Business is now booming for everyone in your industry. Your employer's largest competitor offered you a 10% raise over what you are making now. What do you do?
2. Should a publically held company be loyal to its employees even if it means reduced shareholder value?
3. What are cost-effective ways of letting the people in your sphere of influence know that you care about them and support them?

CHAPTER ELEVEN

Gentleness

"I CHOOSE GENTLENESS. Nothing is won by force. If I raise my voice, may it be only in praise. If I clench my fist, may it be only in prayer. If I make a demand, may it only be of myself." Max Lucado, *Grace for the Moment.*

Debra Stokes

"How did you end up at the University of Alabama?" I asked Debra.

I actually like Ralph Stoke's wife better than I like Ralph—everybody does. Debra is cool. Ralph is very limited—he talks and plays golf. And when he is talking, he is probably talking about playing golf.

Debra likes to do other stuff—drink wine, go on walks, and engage in a variety of discussions. She has the ability to sit still for more than 20 seconds without having to jump up and run around the house.

Debra and Ralph are a little younger than Linda and me, but not much. In the early 1970s, it was a big deal to be African-American and go to a traditionally all-white, southern institution.

Ralph's story is pretty well documented and talked about. What about Debra? As long as we had known one another, I had never asked her the question about how she ended up at the Capstone.

She answered, "Because some guidance counselor at Abbeville High School said my only two choices were Alabama State or, if my parents had a lot of money, Tuskegee—they are both black colleges." She wanted to major in journalism, and she felt the University of Alabama was the best school for that major.

As a young girl, Debra admired prominent African-American black women, such as Shirley Chisholm (who was the first African-American woman elected to Congress), Barbara Jordon (from Texas), and Michelle Clark (who was a news reporter).

Debra was a voracious reader of books and did well in school. She earned a National Merit Scholarship to Auburn University but turned it down because they did not have a school for journalism. She was quite thankful for that, as she would have never met Ralph had she gone to Auburn.

Something did not make sense. She received a National Merit Scholarship from a rural school in Alabama? That was not my perception of the Alabama school system, especially in the late 1960s early 1970s.

She then told me that she went to grades 1-8 in an all-black school. The school was Free Gift Elementary, which was run by Free Gift AME church. I voiced my concerns about her educational background.

"Oh, John, the black school was much better than the white school. Those black teachers understood how important education was, and they worked us to death. They also learned to do more with less resources." she said.

I always learn something when I talk with my friend, Debra.

When desegregation and forced busing came, the best black students were selected to go to Abbeville High. In her graduation class at Abbeville, there were only four students who were accepted and went to the University of Alabama—two black kids and two white kids.

Ralph, like many of my friends and me, married way over his head. Debra is a jewel.

While Ralph was still getting his beauty sleep, Debra and I took a walk around Marietta.

Debra currently works for a member of the Georgia House of Representatives. The congresswoman takes great pride in telling people, including Debra, that she represents a very affluent area around Atlanta. One day, the congresswoman left something at the office. She mentioned this to Debra, and Debra offered to bring it to her.

The response was, "Oh no. I would not want you driving over here from the Southside. She had made the assumption that, because Debra was black, she lived on the south side of Atlanta.

Debra replied, "No problem. I am one of your neighbors; I can run it right over."

Now that is funny. I would have loved to have seen that congresswoman's face.

When I was thinking through this book, I recalled that discussion on our Marietta walk. I needed someone for the "peace" fruit. Debra was going to be an ideal candidate because she was African-American, went to the University of Alabama, lived in the south all of her life, and had to deal with obnoxious white people like that congress lady. So naturally, Debra forgave all of those folks. What a perfect "peace" model she would make.

I set up a phone conversation to validate my thoughts.

I asked my friend to pick up where she decided she was not going to an all-black college thinking that surely there was some drama getting into Alabama.

She said, "Well, let me see—I took the SAT's, the ACT's and sent in an application and got accepted."

That's it? I thought—too simple. Surely there is more to the story.

"So tell me about Alabama," I said.

Again, I am listening for the opening to pounce on the social injustice issue. Surely there are some great stories on how she was discriminated against and how, in heroic fashion, she forgave them, I thought.

Debra replied, "I picked journalism, was madly in love with Ralph, and dropped out my junior year to get married and move with him to Greenville, South Carolina. Then I came back to school for a year and graduated."

Now I was getting desperate because this was not going the way I thought it would. Oh, by the way, I know Debra well enough to know that she obviously knew what I was digging for and she may have been messing with me a little. I think she wanted me to figure all this out for myself. She missed her calling—she should have been a teacher for people with dense heads.

"Okay, then tell me about this legislature stuff," I said. I was now desperate for some good stories on forgiving people.

Debra went on to say, "I have always prayed for our legislature. An opportunity came up for me to work part-time, so I took it. I would be able to walk the halls and offices and pray in person."

Bingo—I was wrong again, and the light began to flicker in my head.

I can see Debra doing that—praying for those people without them even knowing it.

"Gentleness" is what came to mind. Debra would reflect a wonderful example of gentle behavior. When I was talking with Linda about this, Linda said, "Debra is the gentlest person I have ever met."

The Max Lucado description of gentleness defines Debra. Gentleness or humility does not mean weakness. Again, it is the opposite of weakness; it is strength.

Debra ended our conversation and said, "Sure, I have had people discriminate against me and treat me different because I am black and a woman. However, I also felt that was their problem and not mine, so I just ignored it."

Nathan

My name is Nathan, which means "God has given" in Hebrew. I was the prophet during the time of King David and also of King David's son, Solomon.

To understand me and why the Holy Spirit helped me with gentleness, one needs to understand more of who I had to deal with—King David.

David is the fellow that, in his youth, slayed Goliath with a slingshot. He was very much a "doer" and had what one today would call a "Type A" behavior. He was very outgoing, and some would say almost aggressive. There was never a dull moment around this king.

He was loved by his followers and hated by his enemies. History painted him in a good light. Today, if you travel to Israel on El Al, the first-class section is referred to as the "King David section." He won many battles and did many great things as king. He was also the author of many of the Psalms.

However, he was also responsible for one of the most heinous acts of abuse of power in world history. Here is the story.

We were at war with the Amorites, and our army was in the field. David was not with the army, which was unusual behavior for a king. The people expected their king to lead them in battle, so this particular event started off on the wrong foot. David should have been with his soldiers.

One evening, David looked down from his balcony and saw a woman of amazing beauty. His passion for her burned, and he summoned his aides to bring her to him. That evening, he made love to her, and she became pregnant. Bathsheba was the wife of one of David's soldiers, Uriah, who was fighting for David in the field at the time.

In an effort to cover up his adulterous deed, David sent word for Uriah to come home for some rest and relaxation (R&R), figuring that if he also made love to his wife, the indiscretion would never be discovered. However, Uriah felt it would be unfair for him to enjoy the pleasures of his wife while the other men slept in their tents awaiting battle, so he did not sleep with his wife. David even tried getting Uriah drunk so he might let his guard down and make love to his wife. The soldier still refrained.

What David finally did was send a note back to Uriah's commanding officer, instructing him to put Uriah at the head of the attack and to then withdraw support so Uriah would be killed. That is exactly what happened. Now David could add murder to his list of bad deeds.

David went on to marry Bathsheba. I guess David figured he had gotten away with the crime.

Sometimes, being God's prophet is a real difficult and (perhaps) even dangerous job. This was one of those times, as God put it on my heart to confront the king on this sin.

An "in your face" approach with King David might have gotten me killed, as David was volatile, to say the least. I think the fruit of gentleness was one of the reasons we got along so well.

I needed to get David to come to grip with what he had done. I chose to tell him a parable that went something like this: There was once a rich man and a poor man. The rich man had lots of possessions and plenty of livestock. The poor man only had a ewe lamb that he had purchased. He treated the lamb like a member of his family, feeding her from the table and cuddling with her. He loved the ewe lamb very much.

The rich man was expecting a guest, but he did not want to slaughter one of his own herd for the feast. He did the unthinkable and killed the poor man's ewe to feed his guest.

When I told David this story, he was beside himself with anger towards the rich man. His volatile nature was evident, and he demanded to know who the rich man was so he could punish him. I let his anger swell, and then I quietly said, "It is you. You are that rich man."

David wept, and wept, and cried out to God in remorse, and asked for forgiveness.

I can see my sister, Debra Stokes, gently chiding members of the state legislature in Georgia in such a manner that is equally productive.

Comment

I think those who can display the fruit of gentleness are able to deliver tough news to people in power or to anyone for that matter. The correction that Nathan delivered to David about Uriah and Bathsheba was not the only tough news that he delivered. God also used Nathan to approach David about building a temple, a place for God, and gave him the disheartening news that David's son, Solomon, was God's choice to build the temple.

I was the beneficiary of a man that reflected the fruit of gentleness. Jim Tisheur was a plant manager who worked for me when I was Vice President of Operations with the Gilman Company in Chattanooga, Tennessee. I was in my early 30s at the time and full of vim and vinegar. I am impatient by nature. Add in some youth on top of that, and I might have been somewhat of a handful.

Occasionally, I would have a kneejerk reaction and come up with a decision or an idea that probably would have been harmful. Jim never came right out and said that what I was fixing to do was stupid. In his own gentle manner, he would ask questions to let me discover my stupidity for myself. I really appreciated Jim and his gentle approach to me. I have since learned that having such a person on your team is very rare. Many times, people tell the boss what they think the boss wants to hear, and they definitely will not address problems that the boss is causing.

It is easy to be gentle when everything is going right and smooth. Gentleness really counts in tough situations.

One is more approachable when reflecting gentleness. If you were the boss, wouldn't you like to be more approachable so people are open with you about their concerns?

Discussion

1. Discuss a time when you needed to deliver really bad news or criticism to a superior.
2. How did it go? Would you do anything different?
3. In what ways can you develop gentleness so that you can reflect it?

CHAPTER TWELVE
Self-Control

"I CHOOSE SELF-CONTROL. I am a spiritual being. After my body is dead, my spirit will soar. I refuse to let what will rot rule the eternal. I will be drunk only by joy. I will be impassioned only by my faith. I will be influenced only by God. I will be taught only by Christ." Max Lucado, *Grace for the Moment.*

Pastor Jim Farmer

"Is this going to be a five or a seven-lap sermon?" asked my friend, Gene Cuzzart.

Jim Farmer looked a little confused at the question. Jim, who is over six feet tall, towered over Gene and me as we chatted in our fellowship hall before our 9:30 a.m. church service.

When Jim preached, he used no notes. Our altar was a big square, with pews surrounding three sides and the choir facing the fourth side. During his sermon, Jim would walk around the altar so he could look at everyone. It was a slow pace, and he did a lot of pausing. An average sermon—twenty minutes or so, would be about four to five laps. If Jim was really excited, he might go up to six or seven laps. Gene would count the laps. My friend, Gene, might be somewhat of a geek.

Jim is a Marine Corps Vietnam Combat Veteran. That was his path to affording a college education, to earn the GI bill.

He had come from a dysfunctional family. Only the warmth and love of a neighbor family showed him what family life and relationships should be like. In addition to showing him the love they would their own son, they introduced him to church life, which made a strong impression on the young man.

College was behind him, and he was "living the life." As a successful sales manager for a manufacturing company, he was earning more money than he could ever imagine. However, at age 30, he got that "call from God" that you hear so many pastors talk about.

The "call of the world" was also quite strong. It takes a lot of self-control to take your hand off of the steering wheel and let God drive the car. I asked Jim if it was like a "Damascus Road Experience," like that of the Apostle Paul.

"No, it was gradual. Probably a five-year process," he replied.

I first met Jim when Chesapeake Consulting was doing a large project for Bishop John Schol and the Baltimore-Washington Conference of the United Methodist Church. At the time, Jim was on the Bishop's staff.

Like in most churches, the constraint of the institution was spiritual leadership—pastors that had the ability to connect people with God and lead a staff and congregation. There were not enough of these spiritual leaders in the conference to go around, and retirement of many was on the horizon. We mentioned to Bishop Schol that he had a bunch of excellent spiritual leaders at the conference center and that he should get them out from behind a desk and put them into the field, leading congregations. By the way—that is where they would rather be anyway.

As luck would have it, Pastor Farmer was assigned to Severna Park United Methodist, where my family and I attended. Jim asked if I would serve as chair of our church council, so I was able to work closely with him, and we became good friends.

When I thought of the fruit of self-control, one of the things that popped into my head was physical fitness and taking care of oneself. I immediately thought of Jim and Bishop Schol, as both are runners and keep themselves pretty fit. However, the longer I discussed this book/project with Jim, the more he helped me to realize that perhaps self-control is more about listening to the voice of the Holy Spirit and ignoring the voice of the world.

The voice of the world comes to us through the words and actions of other people who are reacting to our behavior.

Severna Park UMC was a sick church when he took over. The previous pastor left on bad terms and attendance, morale, and vitality had nosedived. Attendance was at a 30-year low although the community had increased in population. Doing things the same way was not going to work. However, as we all know, changing things was going to be met with resistance. The world is leading the resistance when it comes to improving the church—the body of Christ. Pastor Jim was steadfast in listening to and obeying God.

Jim had grown churches before, and he already had, in his mind, some of what he wanted to do. There are steps to making disciples. I have seen these named a variety of things; all are about the same. Jim's steps were invite, nurture, and serve. People are invited into the church and establish a relationship with Christ. That relationship is nurtured through small groups and Bible studies, and then the disciples are sent out to serve in some manner—being the hands and feet of Christ in the world. Jim assigned each of those areas to one of his associate pastors. He expected them to report and be accountable for progress. There was enormous resistance to this change. However, Jim never wavered and (in his gentle manner) saw the change through to success. He was not listening to the world tell him how he should not do this.

Bishop John Schol had a similar situation. He was taking over from a bishop that had let the conference decline, and the financial situation was in bad shape. Keeping the same leaders and policies was not an option if he expected the conference to improve. Bishop Schol listened to the Holy Spirit and not listen to those resisting change.

Prophet Jeremiah

"Ah, Lord God! Behold, I do not know how to speak, for I am only a youth."

That was my response when God informed me he was "appointing" me as a prophet to the nation. I was too young. No one was going to listen to me.

However, you know how it is when God wants you to do something; he also equips you.

Eventually, I was credited with writing these books: Kings, Lamentations, and (of course) the book that is named after me. I could not have done all of this writing were it not for the help of my disciple and scribe, Baruch ben Neriah.

I lived during a very bad time in our history. Many of our people were worshipping Baal and had forsaken God. My job was to point out the errors of their ways, encourage them to repent, and foretell what was ahead. Exile was ahead, and no one wanted to hear all of this bad news.

I literally cried out in agony so much that I was referred to as the "Weeping Prophet."

I saw our temple destroyed and our people being taken into exile in Babylon. Everything that I preached was unpopular, and many threatened me. It would have been so easy just to get along or not to preach at all. This is where that self-control thing came into play. I had to only listen to God, not the ways of the world.

Like Jim Farmer, I needed to stay the course and listen to the voice of God and not the voices of the world.

Comment

When I look over these reflections of the fruit of self-control, I sense that this is a fruit that is needed most in times of change and turmoil. Things are in chaos, and being in alignment with what God would have is paramount. There are voices all over, and the leader needs to discern and pick the one he or she must listen to.

I struggled to come up with engaging thoughts while writing about this fruit. To try and clear my mind, I read the book of Jeremiah. As I read the book, I almost got the sense that Jeremiah was alone on an island, with only God to talk with. Everyone was against him, and no one wanted to hear the message he was bringing. Other prophets were preaching more about good news and were discounting what the young Jeremiah was saying. He got death threats, and it had to have been difficult staying the course and obeying what God was telling him to say.

I recall feeling concerned for Bishop Schol as he led the Baltimore-Washington Conference of The United Methodist Church through much-needed change. Although the bishop was new to the conference, most of the other leaders had been there for their entire career. Some of these leaders transitioned out of leadership roles and would lose "power and influence" under a different culture. A significant number of the transitioning leaders turned on Bishop Schol and (in my opinion) were downright mean to him in word and in action. It was not a pleasant thing to observe in the church. However, he stayed the course and did not waver.

After eight years, Bishop Schol was assigned to another conference, and many of the existing powerbrokers returned to the former culture that lacked accountability.

Bishop Schol is now settled in that other conference (and doing a marvelous job by the way). I never heard Bishop Schol complain about the way he was treated.

It might have been easier for Jim Farmer and John Schol to listen to the words of the world instead of the voice of the Holy Spirit.

Many times, people look to their leaders on how to model their own behavior. If the leader lacks self-control, what type of an example is that? Jim Farmer, John Schol, and Jeremiah did an excellent job.

Discussion

1. Describe a time in your experience when there was great change going on, and you needed to make choices.
2. What decision criteria did you use?
3. How can one ferret out the voices of the world from the voice of God?

CHAPTER THIRTEEN

Action Plan to Keep the Cows Milked

LET US REVIEW our leadership triangle again.

Chesapeake Leadership Model

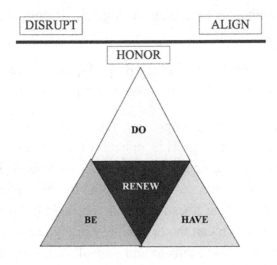

The "Renew" part of the triangle is the most important part and is the one that requires the focus. All other parts of the triangle are an effect of "Renew." That is to say, if you focused on "Renew," "Have" and "Be" will improve, making a much more effective

"Do." It is sort of like the old saying: what goes into your head, gravitates to your heart, and comes out in your hands (behavior). If you focus on what goes in your head (reading, TV, music, conversation, social media, etc.), all should work out well. The issue is the focus of your time.

There are four aspects of "Renew"—physical, social, mental and spiritual. All can be driven off of the spiritual aspect. Now we are really getting focused.

Let us start with physical: "You should know your body is a temple for the Holy Spirit who is in you. You have received the Holy Spirit from God. So you do not belong to yourself." 1 Corinthians 6:19

When you look at your physical body as the home and dwelling place of God—the Holy Spirit, it creates a much more serious meaning about taking care of yourself. It puts me on a bit of a guilt trip.

Getting a physical, eating properly, and getting the proper amount of rest and exercise are important parts of "Renewal."

The social aspect is improving relationships with those in your sphere of influence. This sphere of influence would include relatives, friends, neighbors, and work associates. I feel this also involves the idea of being able to be spontaneous with relationships. That does not mean "oh, let's go to the beach on a whim;" it does mean that, perhaps, while you are rushing through the plant that you manage and one of your employees acts like they want to talk, take the time to stop and be social—engage. We are meant to be in relationships—so be in relationships.

The mental part does include keeping your mind active, perhaps by working puzzles and reading. When you crank in the spiritual component, it means reading and looking at the right things. Again, what goes into your head gravitates to your heart. There is an old computer phrase: "garbage in; garbage out." The same is true for us.

Spiritual renewal is based on the "means of grace."

Grace is something that is unearned; God gives it to us. However, God did not intend for us to lull around, waiting to experience grace. He wants us to engage in what John Wesley referred to as "the means of grace."

John Wesley is the Englishman who is credited with founding the Methodist Church. The term "Methodist" comes from people referring to the followers as people who did things in a certain "method."

One can almost make the means of grace complicated. I am going to try and boil it down to several action items that will encompass piety and mercy and address both individual and corporate activities.

1. You need to attend weekly worship. Our God wants to be worshiped and loved, and He cherishes us telling Him how much we love Him. Singing songs of praise and thanksgiving should be part of any worship experience. It should be a joyous occasion.
2. Daily prayer, Bible reading, meditation and spiritual/devotional reading. I try and pray several times throughout the day to keep grounded. God wants to talk with you. This is how you dial Him up.
3. Fasting. Before you go out and start starving yourself to death, consider doing some research on fasting. A meaningful fast brings you closer to God.

4. Meeting with other Christians on an ongoing basis to discuss how God is working in your life. It could be a small group or an accountability group.
5. Bible study.
6. Partaking of the sacraments.
7. Addressing issues of mercy and justice. Going to visit those who are sick or in prison. Sticking up for the less fortunate, working in a soup kitchen.

How do you take these renewal issues and turn them into reality? In my opinion, you must schedule your time well. Life is nothing more than time. You have an 85% better chance of something actually happening if you write it down.

I am going to share with you what has worked for me. Are there other ways to do this? Of course, there are other ways. This is just the one that has evolved for me.

The tool I use is the *Franklin Planner*. The version I use has two pages for each day—on the left page, there are lines for daily tasks, and down that same side is a breakdown of the day into hours. On the right-hand side, there is a blank page for notes.

Using the left page, I segment the upcoming day into five sections:

- Before work
- From the time I arrive at work to time for lunch break
- Lunch time
- After lunch until quitting time
- After quitting time

I line these sections off in my planner, and then I will populate these sections of the day with numbers that relate to my task items.

For each day, I have a list of tasks. Here is a typical day, which I took from Wednesday, August 31, 2016.

1. Have lunch with Greg
2. Exercise
3. Complete information for bank
4. Spiritual (this is a devotional by the Upper Room)
5. Aerobic (normally an hour walk with the dog)
6. Spiritual 2 (This is the morning devotional from Max Lucado's book, *Grace for the Moment*)
7. Water—I have three containers of water I want to drink each day, so I put it on my task list.
8. Write Joy—this is a young lady I help sponsor in Kenya
9. Spiritual 3 (this is the afternoon devotional from Max's book)
10. Work on new book (this one as a matter of fact)
11. Pray—I put this on my day in three different time periods.
    a. In the morning before work. At this time, in addition to giving God praise, I go over my prayer list, which includes that prayer of Jabez that we mentioned and also the Lord's Prayer.
    b. When I first get to work, I pray over my tasks list for the day.
    c. In the afternoon, I pray a prayer of thanksgiving for the many blessings (next to my itemized prayer list, there is an itemized blessing list that gets added to during the month).
12. Plan tomorrow's day
13. Contact Pac Man (one of the young men we mentored at the Naval Academy, who is having dog behavior problems)
14. Contact Drew—young man I mentor, who is a missionary
15. Attend small-group coaches meeting
16. Get a haircut

17. Make sales touches scheduled for that day.
18. Go on mini walks (go around the block at work)
19. Work on content for our website
20. Whole 30 meals—a certain diet I am on that, for the most part, eliminates sugar and flour.

These are the numbers I use to populate the segments of the days. If the item is critical to be done, I put it in a circle. If it can be pushed out or is not real important or urgent, I put it in a small square.

As the day progresses, I scratch through the circles and squares.

Why this level of detail? Doesn't it limit you?

First of all, when you plan and use your time well, it actually frees time and capacity for the unexpected. I find I have MORE time for spontaneity and dealing with the unexpected. Also, the moment is the only thing that matters. We cannot do anything about yesterday, and tomorrow is certainly not guaranteed. What we are doing now matters.

God has given us the gift of time, and He expects a return. Making a daily plan to use time wisely is a good thing.

SUMMARY

This Moment Counts

THE SUN HAD JUST RISEN over Shipley's Elementary School in Millersville, Maryland, and it is only Maggie, my German shepherd Diva-Dog, and me in the large athletic field. It is tempting to blow this off—not do it. Who is going to know the difference? Maggie is not going to tell, especially if I bribe her with a dog cookie.

"Eighteen, Sir," I shouted to the non-existent Drill Sargent. I had just finished my 18th pushup. Pushups were the last of my seven (the Biblical number of completion) exercises. It was the 18th day of Lent, and I had committed to doing my annual Lent exercises, so each day, I add a repetition per day, up to forty. Lent is a special time of year and is one of several times where it is common to plan, reflect, and discern—all of which are good things. My Lent exercises are something someone half my age should be doing, and me doing them is not a pretty sight. They consist of jumping jacks, lunges, jumps, a back exercise, squats, sit-ups, and the dreaded pushups, which I save until last.

What I do in the moment is important. I can talk myself into thinking I will do them when I get to my hotel room in Kearney, Nebraska later that day. Of course, I won't. I will want to relax with my colleagues, talk shop, and watch the NCAA tournament.

This moment matters. I will not get it back, so it's "eighteen, Sir," and I am done for the day.

I am going to wrap-up this book by relaying another experience I had at the Bibb County Correctional Facility. In our small group, we were talking about the need for someone to have a vision of what they wanted to be and to accomplish. In the context of our discussion, this vision is one that came from discernment and was from God.

About eight of us in the group were pondering this thought when David Files spoke up. David has been in prison since 2008 and is serving a life sentence for murder. He had become a Christian nine months earlier and has immersed himself in scripture, study, prayer, and worship life.

"You need to make sure the devil does not turn that vision that is in your mind into a permanent daydream," David said.

Where did that come from? I thought. That was really profound and deep.

David's words of wisdom have shed an entirely new light on daydreams. They are no longer a good thing in my mind. I need to act on them unless I want to make the devil a happy camper.

What you do now with this moment is critical. You are not going to get it back.

You may decide to change some of how you approach things based on some things that this book may have sparked. You may also want to act on that vision you are pondering. If so—begin your journey now. And enjoy the trip!

PRAISE FOR *COWS DON'T STAY MILKED*

"A wise preacher once said, 'A breakdown in leadership is usually a breakdown in character.' We see the reality of that wise observation daily in almost all areas of our life. John Covington's book is not only an excellent read on how to be a more effective leader but if you read this book carefully and prayerfully you will begin to see the keys to developing true godly character in your life. Developing character is the key to sustaining effective leadership as you attempt to influence others. John's book is entertaining, insightful and possibly life-changing for some. Hope you will read and enjoy."
Keith Pugh, Senior Pastor Alberta Baptist, Alberta City, Alabama

"*Cows Don't Stay Milked*" highlights the fact that great leaders differentiate themselves by constantly invoking the facets of their faith as they touch and mentor others on their journey."
H. Dean McClure, President TTL, Inc.

"There are many leadership books and articles available. John Covington has accomplished something unique in his new book *Cows Don't Stay Milked*. John has demonstrated how integral love and its subordinates are to our souls, our relationships and our life's mission of Love, live and lead."
Michael Storms, Director of Operations, Elliott Group

"By sharing adventures of modern day and biblical leaders, John Covington gives us a special unique book on how to enhance our leadership skills. *Cows Don't Stay Milked* is an engaging, easy-to-read book filled with humor and poignant stories. Throughout

123

these stories, we see examples of how choosing our attitudes have a profound impact on our outlook and the outlook of those we lead. Reading the book will not only give you a pause; it should improve your approach to leadership and life."
Karen Baldwin, Vice President Development, The University of Alabama (retired)

"*Cows Don't Stay Milked* kept me captivated page after page. Each story about a real human living out Holy Spirit character inspired and intrigued me. The chapters gave me hope but also some practical tips for living more fully in the authenticity of Holy character. I highly recommend that all leaders give John's book a read. It would also be a fantastic study for any small group, but especially Christian business leaders."
Diane Kucala, President and Founder of Blueprint Leadership

"As I progressed through John's latest book, *Cows Don't Stay Milked*, it helped reinforce the importance of putting people first in all areas of life. The use of both personal and biblical examples really helped bring the book alive. I recommend this book to anyone, not just related to leadership skills, but in becoming more open minded to the views and the experiences of others."
Roger Townsend, President/General Manager, Chief Industries Agricultural Division

"John's new book is both an easy read and inspirational. I was able to apply the principles immediately to a current situation. I loved the way he put Biblical characters in a story format. I was honored that our company was mentioned in the book." Wayne Pitchford,
Vice-President of Operations, Neptune Technologies

CPSIA information can be obtained
at www.ICGtesting.com
Printed in the USA
FSOW03n1843260217
31162FS